THE JOY OF BEING SINGLE

THE JOY OF
BEING SINGLE

*Stop Putting Your Life on Hold
and Start Living!*

JANICE HARAYDA

DOUBLEDAY & COMPANY, INC.
Garden City, New York
1986

Library of Congress Cataloging in Publication Data

Harayda, Janice.
    The joy of being single.

    Includes index.
    1. Single people—United States—Life skills guides.
I. Title.
HQ800.4.U6H37   1986   305'.90652   85-10387
ISBN 0-385-23271-3

Portions of the book first appeared in *Glamour* magazine

To Donald M. Murray,
a singular writing teacher,
  and
In grateful memory of
Michele Kamisher (1950–79)

ACKNOWLEDGMENTS

Many of the ideas in this book began to germinate in the 1970s, when I was an editor of *Glamour*. At the magazine I was lucky enough to be able to write repeatedly about single men and women when their numbers were increasing dramatically—to be present at the creation of a major social force. Even more significantly, I was encouraged to write about single people in my own voice and out of my own experience. I am grateful to all the *Glamour* colleagues who supported those early efforts and particularly to Phyllis Starr Wilson, Carol E. Rinzler, Wenda Wardell Morrone, Aimee Ball, and Flora Davis. Above all, however, I am indebted to Ruth Whitney, who remains the magazine's editor in chief. She didn't just approve many of my ideas for articles but contributed her own, including a suggestion for one especially memorable article about single people and food with photos of the naked shelves of their refrigerators —a display that made its point far more effectively than words could have.

Before arriving at *Glamour*, I had other teachers, bosses, and mentors whose imprint my work still bears. They include Frances Koltun, David Butwin, Horace Sutton, Jon Kellogg, Chuck Triblehorn, Richard Wieland, Ralph Williamson, and Eunice Davidson, all early and fine influences. And no one has had a greater impact than Donald M. Murray of the University of New Hampshire English Department, whose *A Writer Teaches Writing* (Houghton Mifflin,

1985) is still the first book I turn to for a professional inspiration. Like many Boston writers, I am also grateful to Dan Wakefield for his continuing affirmation that writers don't just flourish outside New York—they prevail.

Once I had begun writing this book, I was aided in countless ways by Katy Koontz, my research assistant; Mel Berger, my agent; Robert S. Frank, Jr., my lawyer; Susan Schwartz, my editor, and Katharine Phillips, her assistant; and Christine Bodger of ADS Secretarial Services, who labored cheerfully through the typing of many barely legible drafts.

Finally, it is simply myth that single people can get by with "a little help from their friends." They need a lot of help, and no one has provided more than Hans, Phyllis, Warren, and Robert Heilbronner. Dennis Frenchman was the only friend who had the nerve to say, upon learning that I was writing a book that included my personal experiences: "Make me the bright spot." Should there be any doubt in the matter, he is.

For other acts of grace and kindness during the writing of this book or the period leading up to it, I am thankful to Sally Abrahms, Sally Brewster, the Rev. Philip A. C. Clarke, Jean E. Collins, Nancy Davis, Amy Greenhill, Heidi Hampson, Rick Hampson, Judy Rice Millon, Susan Stobaugh Samuelson, Barbara Schiappa, Karen Cord Taylor, Leslie Tweeton, Richard E. Welch III, Jane C. Williams, and Ron Winslow. I am also grateful for the continuing support of my grandmother, Elsie Birdsall; and to the memory of my father, John Harayda; of my godparents, Henrietta Gantner and Matthew Pietrucha; and of my friend and fellow journalist, Michele Kamisher.

Without all of the people listed above, this book might have been possible . . . but it wouldn't have been nearly so much fun.

Bless them all.

"It makes perfect sense to me that people would want to be married. But for me, security is not knowing what's going to happen. Because if I don't know, it could be terrific."

Gloria Steinem

CONTENTS

THE JOY OF BEING SINGLE

Introduction

No matter who you are, where you live, what you look like, or why you are reading these words, one thing can be said about you with certainty: you were born single. You didn't come into this world possessed of a spouse—and it is increasingly likely that you won't leave it with one, either. Today, more than sixty million Americans are unmarried, separated, divorced, or widowed, and their numbers show no signs of diminishing. A generation ago, a man or woman who hadn't wed by age twenty-one might justifiably have felt like a candidate for *Ripley's Believe It or Not;* now someone who has wed may feel the same way. Marriage may still be the norm, but it is increasingly less normative. Singlehood is—and always will be—the universal human condition.

As the numbers of single people have increased, so have their freedoms. Young or old, they can enjoy the rewards of the women's movement, the sexual revolution, and laws that have given them the same right as married people have to buy houses, condos, and co-ops. Being single is no longer a social disease but a fact of life for one out of every three American adults. And for many it is far more than that: it is a wonderful way to get to know themselves before deciding to spend a lifetime getting to know someone else.

Yet, though the stigma attached to being single has all but disappeared, a lot of unattached people act as though it hasn't. The view persists that the abundant life can exist only within a marriage or at least within what is so unromantically called "a relationship." Often single people seem to live in a state of suspended animation, as though waiting for marriage to be delivered by Federal Express. They put off doing countless things they want to—and do many others they don't—in the belief that their marital status leaves them no choice. Their real lives, they tell themselves, will begin when they get married.

The tendency to live in limbo before marriage cuts across lines of age, sex, and personal history. You see it in unmarried women in their twenties who don't save money, because they believe they will one day find a man who will relieve them of having to worry about financial security. You see it in divorced men in their forties who don't have friends over for dinner because they have never learned how to cook. And you see it in men and women in their thirties who take far fewer vacations than they would like to, because they believe they have no one to travel with. All are passing up pleasures they could have right now, hoping that a wedding will one day make up for what they have missed en route to the altar.

A flood tide of recent books and articles about being single has reinforced the idea that life before marriage doesn't really count. In fact, many of them aren't about being single at all. They are about how to get out of being single and into a lifetime partnership, whether you are ready or not. A lot of the recent drivel about the "fear of intimacy" in one sex or the other is simply a new way of telling unattached men and women that they are still not up to speed. A generation ago, single people were relentlessly told by psychiatrists and others that they were "immature." Now they hear that they are "afraid" of "commitment." (Never mind that—in an age when fifty percent of all first marriages and nearly sixty percent of all *second* marriages will end in divorce—a little fear of commitment is downright healthy.) Little has really changed except for the terminology with which single people are sold short. One result is that, though the pressure to marry immediately has diminished, the pressure to marry eventually remains as strong as ever. Single people used to feel obligated to wed; they now feel compelled to "have a relationship" that might lead to marriage someday if not soon. In some cases, one tyranny has merely been exchanged for another.

And there is something else wrong with the new backlash against being single. At a time when traditional sex roles are disappearing, a lot of the new propaganda only serves to keep alive ideas that ought to have been buried with the hoop skirt. Single women aren't called spinsters anymore, but slick city magazines still portray them as lonely and frustrated losers who can do little except listen to their "biological clock" ticking away as though it were Big Ben. Single men past the age of thirty are no longer widely assumed to be gay, but books and articles still depict many as victims of a "Peter Pan syndrome" that keeps them from growing up.

Nobody can deny how wonderful it is to love and be loved for a lifetime. But marriage has never been right for all people, all of the time, and it may not be right for you. Some people just aren't very good at being married, and others who would be good may not have a chance to exercise their skill. So it never makes sense to put your life on hold just because you're single. It makes sense instead to create for yourself the richest, fullest life possible—one that you may or may not someday share with somebody else.

This book is about how to create that sort of life for yourself, whether you are young or old, male or female, never married or several times divorced. It is based on the belief that happiness, whether you are married or single, isn't something you *find* so much as something you *claim:* on your own, for your own. Happiness is also something you earn, in marriage or outside it.

The one thing nobody ever tells you about being single is that, although it can be far *better* than it was a generation ago, it isn't necessarily *easier.* Being single is a job not unlike that of President of the United States, a position from which there is no time off. The buck always stops with you. A single man or woman needs to be his or her own nurse, cook, housekeeper, social director, sex therapist, interior designer, and career counselor—all jobs a married one can sometimes transfer to a spouse.

Even at its best, being single is a far cry from the endless romp on the Big Rock Candy Mountain that the media have sometimes portrayed it to be. An unattached man or woman doesn't just have to answer the same big questions everybody else does about how to make a real difference in an increasingly depersonalized world. A single person also has to face lots of petty annoyances a married person might not. Life can be a little like playing tennis: a singles game tends to be *more* work than doubles, because you have to cover more territory on your own. But that needn't make it any less enjoyable or good for you. Neither would you face fewer challenges if you were married. Life always requires trade-offs. If you were to marry tomorrow, your life would become easier in some ways and harder in others.

This book, of course, doesn't aim to prove the superiority of singlehood over marriage. Rather, it is based on a too rarely acknowledged fact: neither marriage nor singlehood is inherently preferable to the other, but everything depends on what you make of what you have. A good single life can be far better for you than a bad marriage, and it can even be better than a good one, should you find yourself able to give more to the world without a spouse than with one. Some people have compared being married to going through life with a copilot who helps you navigate through difficulty. But being married can also be like going through life with a backseat driver who makes you a little crazy. At times you may do better without either form of company.

Being single is, ultimately, a very personal matter, which is why this book draws on many personal experiences. Midway through my biblically allotted "threescore years and ten," I have spent half a lifetime doing a solo run. Had I married in my teens or twenties, I would no doubt have missed a lot of heartache. But I would also have missed a lot of fun I couldn't have had any other way. And I have covered enough social and geographic territory to know that my own experiences weren't peculiar to a particular place or set of circumstances. I've lived in a suburb, in a small town, and on the Upper East Side of Manhattan, a neighborhood that could certainly claim the title, if one were to be awarded, of Singles Capital of the U.S.A. Throughout all the changes of address, I have found that doing a solo run can at times be a nightmare. But it can also be a dream, whether you chose singlehood or it chose you.

In writing this book, I've weighed my own experiences against those of the hundreds of men and women I've interviewed as a journalist and editor. My first feature article for a national magazine took the form of a diary of my experiences in Second Avenue singles bars, which appeared in *Glamour,* and I have been writing about single people, off and on, ever since. I have also spoken to singles groups around the country, and the speeches give me something that magazines didn't: immediate feedback on how single men and women feel about their lives right now. As I began to be profiled in newspaper articles as an authority on single adults, I received feedback of another sort, in the form of an outpouring of letters from readers who freely shared their thoughts on everything from sex to Campbell's Chunky Chicken Soup for One. All of these experiences convinced me that it is simply myth that all single people secretly want to be married. Many cherish their independence and wouldn't trade places with their married friends even if they could.

Yet, if not all single people want to be married, many do want to have a lot of the things they might have if they were: love, friendship, a nice home, financial security, and ties to the next generation, to name some of the more common ones. And that is why this book is to a great extent about how to find those things outside of marriage.

Nobody, however, can tell you how to be single. So don't adopt the suggestions on these pages; adapt them to your own life. Try, in any case, to keep two things in mind as you go through these pages:

1. *Marriage, like fame or riches, can rarely be pursued directly.* It tends instead to be the byproduct of pursuing something else that you love, such as work, travel, sports, or friendships. So, by filling your life with people and things you care about, you aren't setting yourself up for a lifetime of singlehood so much as creating the conditions under which an ideal marriage could take place. One of the most valuable things anybody can take into marriage is simply a strong track record for happiness, which you can begin putting together now.

2. *The ideal life would probably be to be married for three days a week and single for four, or single for three days a week and married for four.* That life would give everybody the best of two worlds, each with unique advantages and disadvantages. But I, for one, have never found anybody I could interest in that sort of arrangement, and you aren't likely to either. So it is simply smart, instead of chasing an ideal life that may never be caught, to work with what you've got now. As a Talmudic scholar once wrote: "Happiness isn't having what you want; it's wanting what you have." Whether you want to wed tomorrow, in ten years, or never, you have nothing to gain and everything to lose by waiting for marriage to rescue you, the way Steve McQueen rescued the people trapped inside the glass elevator in *The Towering Inferno.* As the psychologist Marilyn Machlowitz has noted: "No man I know has refused to marry a woman just because she already owns a co-op, a fur

coat or a Cuisinart." Neither has any woman ever refused to marry a man just because he could make duck à l'orange for eight or vacationed in Bermuda instead of his backyard.

The ultimate message of this book, then, is simply this: today counts. The worst thing that can happen to you in life *isn't* that you'll never get married; it's that you won't do the things you want to do or become the person you want to be because you were always waiting for somebody to give you the opportunity you already had. E. M. Forster said: "Only connect." The operative phrase for single people today might be: "Only commit." It almost doesn't matter where or how you make your best effort so much as that you make it at all. You may not be able to commit yourself to the man or woman of your dreams, but you can commit to something or somebody—and preferably to lots of somethings or somebodys. And you can bring to all of them no less hope, energy, and passion than you would to a lifetime partnership. In fact, many of the commitments you make now will bring you no fewer joys than a good marriage would, only different sorts of joys.

If or when you wed, you may have a chance to make a different sort of contribution to the world than you can make now. But your contribution will never be more worth making. Your life may someday be far different from what it is now, but it will never be more important. So, instead of waiting for marriage to rescue you, rescue yourself from the belief that real life can only begin with your wedding day. This is your life, and to miss it isn't just to miss the best show in town—it's to miss the only show.

1

Is Your Life on Hold Just Because You're Single? A Quiz

Americans have a remarkable capacity to postpone living. In an upwardly mobile society, almost everybody wants to be somewhere else. Most people also believe their lives will be better when they get there. Children and teenagers think they will have more fun once they are grown up. College students long to leave the ivory tower and join the "real world." Young mothers look forward to all of the things they will do when their children are in school, and corporate executives to retirement. Almost all of these people have one thing in common: they assume life will someday offer more rewards than it does now.

Different groups tend to defer their happiness in different ways. Corporate executives often put off taking vacations on the grounds that the ultimate vacation, retirement, will come soon enough. (Never mind that heart attacks or other unpleasant surprises may prevent them from reaching it at all.) Young parents may forget that they also need to pay some attention to themselves.

Single people have their own ways of living in limbo.

Some men and women lose themselves in an endless cycle of bar-hopping or party-going, pursuing a partner to the exclusion of almost everything else. Others pursue professional goals so aggressively that they wind up, in effect, married to their work.

Most single people, however, find subtler ways of passing up a rich, fulfilling life. Instead of losing themselves in compulsive activity, they lose themselves in compulsive nonactivity. They live in a state of existential drift, denying themselves even the very real joys available to them now, because they are holding out for what they believe to be the far greater pleasures of marriage. Many forgo a lot of pleasures they believe they would enjoy if they were married, such as putting up a Christmas tree or stocking, eating organized meals, or buying a house. Others pass up the delights they may only be able to savor now, such as backpacking through Europe, cultivating offbeat friendships, or taking the courses that might someday be squeezed out by domestic obligations. Still others insist that they want to wed but don't take the steps that might help them reach their goal, such as losing weight, signing on with a video-dating service, or ditching a destructive romance that crowds out healthier ones. Many are victims of what a minister I know refers to as the "can't do everything so I won't do anything" syndrome. They can't make the big changes in their lives, such as getting married and having children. So they don't make little changes either. The catch is that making a lot of small modifications might add up to a much larger one: they would be living in the present instead of in the future.

Then there exist differences between the sexes that reflect their early socialization. Single men tend to postpone making real homes for themselves, as they might by learning how to cook, entertaining graciously, or buying curtains. Single women are more likely to put off investing their money or at least developing a long-range financial strategy that would someday give them something *to* invest. But neither sex is really better off. After all, it's no more fun to worry about getting pellagra than it is to wonder how much cash you could raise by hocking your exercise bike.

Putting off an important project or two, of course, isn't always harmful. Sometimes deferring a goal is what enables you to reach it at all, because you can't do everything at once.

But how much postponing is too much? How can you tell whether deferring a goal will eventually enable you to reach it more efficiently, or whether it may prevent you from reaching it at all?

The following quiz is intended to help you answer those questions. It covers all of the major categories of actions that single people tend to postpone. But it's not a quiz you can pass or fail so much as one that is intended to help you get a reading on where you stand now and therefore on where you want to go.

1. Did you take at least one week of vacation last year during which you went somewhere other than to see your family?

2. Do you eat at least one hot, balanced meal every day?

3. Did you have a party for your last birthday, even if you had to give it yourself?

4. If you have family heirlooms, such as afghans knit by your grandmother or demitasse spoons from an estate, do you use them?

5. Do you regularly either (a) put up a Christmas tree or (b) light Hanukkah candles?

6. Do you sleep on a real bed instead of a convertible sofa or mattress on the floor?

7. If you believe in God, do you attend religious services?

8. If you wanted to go to see a movie and couldn't find anyone to go with you, would you go to see it alone?

9. Can you realistically envision buying a house or condo within the next five years and are you saving up for it now?

10. Do you freely invite married couples to dinner without feeling obligated to dredge up a date for yourself?

11. Do your married friends invite you to dinner without feeling they have to dredge up someone for you?

12. Is there someone in or near your apartment building on whom you could count to retrieve your mail or water your plants while you are away?

13. If you are a woman, have you ever called a man for a date?

14. If you are a man, have you ever had a woman call you, and been delighted that she did?

15. Do you have deep friendships with people of both sexes?

16. If someone were to open your refrigerator door right now, would he or she see substantially more than six-packs of beer or diet soft drinks and half-empty jars of mustard?

17. Is there at least one child in your life whom you talk to or correspond with regularly and who sees you as an ally?

18. Is there at least one elderly person in your life who views you as a source of joy and comfort in his or her advancing age?

19. Does your home contain framed photos of people who are important to you?

20. Do you also carry pictures of people you love in your wallet?

21. Do you make a real effort to take care of yourself as well as you would if you were married and had someone urging you to? Have you—for instance—seen a dentist within the past eighteen months?

22. Do you also make a real effort to do things you couldn't or wouldn't do if you were married?

23. Have you done as much as you'd like to look attractive to the other sex?

24. Do you cook well enough to be able to have people over to dinner, even at the last minute, without fearing the results?

25. Have you had a lawyer draw up your will?

26. Have you registered to vote in the next election in your town?

27. Within the past year, have you done something to improve the quality of life in your community, such as working on a political campaign or collecting for the United Way?

28. Does your home contain living things, such as plants or pets, that you take pride in tending?

29. Do you have at least a few unmarried friends whom you admire a lot, without feeling in the least sorry for them because they don't have spouses?

30. If you found yourself without dates for longer than felt comfortable, would you feel free to try such things as dating services or the personals ads?

31. Have you moved beyond saving your money to actively investing it?

32. Do you usually date people who are good to you and good for you?

33. If you sprained your ankle and needed to go to an emergency room, would you unhesitatingly ask a friend or neighbor to drive you there, instead of making things worse by struggling into a taxi on your own?

34. Have your family and friends stopped urging you to "settle down"?

35. Within the past year, have you tried at least one or two new activities that you've never enjoyed before?

36. Within the past year, have you gone to at least one or two places that you've never before visited?

37. Do you have at least a few friends to whom you feel as close as you do to your family?

38. Do you have at least one deep and abiding source of satisfaction in your life besides your friends?

39. Do you have at least one deep and abiding source of satisfaction in your life besides your work?

40. Are you currently involved in something that will promote your intellectual growth, such as taking a class or attending a book discussion group?

41. Can you invite people over to your home without feeling embarrassed by it?

42. Do you have people over as often as you would if you were married?

43. Do you carry adequate insurance, including life, health, and auto coverage, plus other kinds as needed?

44. Do you have at least a few people in your life to whom you could talk in a crisis as confidentially as you would to a spouse?

45. Have you overcome any habits that you'd hate to have a prospective mate learn of, such as drinking beer for breakfast or repeatedly overdrawing your checking account?

46. Do you almost always manage to see the humor in catastrophes that befall you?

47. If you could look into a crystal ball and know you'd still be single in ten years, would you nonetheless be glad you'd done things as you had?

48. If you could look into a crystal ball and know you'd marry in a few months, would you nonetheless be glad you'd done things as you had?

49. Can you attend friends' weddings without feeling cheated by life?

50. Can you attend your college reunions without feeling jealous of most of your classmates?

51. Within the past week, have you told somebody that you love him or her?

52. Within the past week, has somebody said that he or she loves you?

53. If having a good sex life is important to you when you are single, do you have that sort of sex life now or know that you've had one in the past?

54. Do at least a few of your married friends—frankly—envy you?

KEY

Nobody can evaluate the above questionnaire better than you can. No matter what your answers, you may know you're happier than ever—or unhappier than you need to be. What follow, therefore, are simply some rough guidelines to help you assess your responses:

1. *Ten or fewer nos:* Congratulations. You have achieved that rare state of being able to live in the present while not neglecting to plan for the future. You may not have everything you want in life just yet, but you are working with what you've got, and sometimes playing it to the hilt. It's likely that some of your married friends *do* envy you, and with reason.

2. *Eleven to twenty-five nos:* Probably it often seems as though you aren't grabbing as much gusto as you could from life, and you may not be sure why. Maybe you've over-invested in one part of life, such as a romance that isn't panning out, while ignoring too many other potential sources of gratification: your home, your friends, your leisure pursuits. Try to cast a wider net, and you may find that changes start occurring almost immediately.

3. *More than twenty-five nos:* It may or may not be true, as the folk saying goes, that life is what happens to you while you are making other plans. But singlehood is what is happening to you while you are making plans for marriage. Why not be good to yourself and live a little in the meantime?

2

Happy Single People Are All Alike

More than a generation ago, when Sigmund Freud was asked to name the ingredients of a happy life, he replied simply: love and work. As all psychoanalysts worthy of their couches know, the good doctor spoke from the perspective of a man who would remain happily married for more than a half century—and whose society could scarcely have dreamed of such things as singles cruises, T.G.I. Fridays, and video dating.

So it isn't surprising that Freud's prescription for the good life often provides little comfort for single people. How can you count on love when you haven't had a decent date in months or find joy in a job you took because it was the only one you could get?

Since Freud's day, many social scientists have found, quite simply, that a happy life is a diverse life. Research increasingly shows that fulfilled people have more than one source of satisfaction and often have many. Love and work matter, but so do many other things. They can include religion, friendship, travel, sports, hobbies, and community service, to name some of the more common. And it's not just romantic love that matters. Even married people need to be sustained by far more than the deep affection they feel for their spouses.

The research into happiness has particular implications for single people. A married person's life, almost by its nature, has diversity. A mate with limited interests still tends to be drawn into those of a spouse. A shy person doesn't lack for companionship when married to someone outgoing. Complementarity is powerful—and also breeds contentment. Lacking the benefits of such marital synergy, single people need to work harder to achieve diversity on their own. Not to do so is to risk leading a life that is stifling in its narrowness, and to long all the more ardently for a spouse who would broaden it.

Apart from looking at what makes people in general happy, many researchers have studied the specific characteristics of happy marriages. But happy single people's lives have received almost no attention at all.

It's almost impossible to pass a magazine stand without spotting a cover story on a subject such as "The Secret of Happy Marriages." It's much harder to find articles on happy single lives. Stories about unattached men and women tend to focus on their problems, such as loneliness, instead of on their joys.

What makes some single people's lives so much happier than others? And how can other unattached adults profit from their example?

To paraphrase Tolstoy, happy single people are all alike, but every unhappy single person is unhappy in his or her own way. Here are some of the common denominators of the former:

I. *Happy single people have close friends of both sexes.*

When I was growing up, people used to say that every single woman needed a few male friends, because you never knew when your toaster might break down and you would need someone to fix it. This idea has always struck me as a great put-down of (a) the ability of my female friends to fix toasters, too; and (b) what friends have to offer besides electrical repair services.

On one level, of course, friends of the other sex *can* help to plug gaps in your everyday survival skills. The first time I lived in a house that did not belong to my parents, for instance, I would have been lost without my next-door neighbor Frank, who was always ready to run over when the boiler blew or a car needed jump starting.

But friends of the other sex can do far more than teach you things your Home Ec teacher somehow neglected. They can also insure that you never lose emotional contact with fifty percent of the human race. After all, there exists a crucial difference between needing *a* man or *a* woman—and needing *men* or needing *women*. And if nobody always needs the former, almost everybody always does need the latter.

Having friends of the other sex adds contrast to your life and a little of the diversity that contributes to happiness. But those friends do something else, and that is to help keep your spirits up. I have never known a single man or woman whose social life had no dry spells, and during them it is easy to believe you have ceased to appeal to the people you want to attract. Then and at other times, friends of the opposite sex remind you that you matter to more than one gender.

Friends of the other sex also give you *hope* for more than one gender. Many single people continually wind up involved with men or women who treat them badly. A powerful antidote can be provided by friends of the other sex who treat you well. Nobody can long remain convinced that there exist no "good" men or women out there when he or she has friends who testify regularly to the contrary. Whenever I am involved with a man whose actions somehow disappoint me, I ask whether I'd put up with the same behavior if it came from a male friend. If I wouldn't, I find, the romance generally goes. In such ways, friends of the other sex can do a lot to help keep your romantic standards high.

Of course, friends of the same sex are vital, too. The great British psychiatrist John Bowlby noted in *Loss* (Basic Books, 1982) that many widows and widowers find it hard to participate in social events involving both sexes, which remind them too forcefully of their loss of a partner. Unmarried and divorced people can feel the same way after the end of an important love affair. Then and at other times, friends of the same sex can be an emotional lifeline.

II. *Happy single people feel connected to a family.*

The ties you acquire to both sexes may begin to feel as significant as blood bonds, which is all to the good. Not many single people live close to the families that nature provided them. So most need others who supply the sort of emotional equity married people find in their spouses.

Some observers insist that single people need a "blended" or "extended" family. I prefer the term "honorary family," which denotes the honor it is to belong to one. Then, too, this sort of group doesn't so much extend your natural family as create a whole new one.

Sometimes you can plug into an existing honorary family. Many churches and synagogues, for example, comprise a ready-made family for their parishioners. Their newsletters list members' birthdays and publicize their promotions. Members visit each other in the hospital and comfort each other in grief. One congregation put together a box of ninety birthday cards for a widow celebrating her ninetieth birthday, each of them individually signed by someone in her church. At another church, the rector pauses during the service to ask who will be celebrating a birthday during the upcoming week. Someone usually comes forward, then stands at the front of the sanctuary as the congregation sings "Happy Birthday," accompanied by the organist. It isn't hard to understand why its members see themselves as a family.

Some companies, too, comprise a sort of family for their employees. In *In Search of Excellence* (Harper & Row, 1982), Thomas J. Peters and Robert H. Waterman, Jr., observe that many of the country's best-run corporations effectively serve this function for their workers. The 3M Company, for one, becomes a sort of second home for many whom it employs. It provides travel, sports, choral, and other clubs in addition to the usual corporate perks. Good for all sorts of employees, such companies can especially benefit single people with no blood relations nearby.

Not everybody, however, can connect with an existing clan. Sometimes it's necessary to piece together a new one by bringing friends together regularly. Four amateur musicians I know of have gotten together one Sunday afternoon a month for years, to play chamber music in one of their living rooms. Having started out as casual acquaintances linked mostly by their love of Bach, the players have melded into a tight family, "there" for music but also for each other. One woman has managed to put together a similarly devoted group by giving regular dinner parties to which she invites the people she likes best.

How a tribe comes together matters less than what it represents: a constellation of people who love you for richer or poorer, for better or worse, and in sickness and in health. This sort of group is so important that you may need to develop several over the years as you move to different addresses.

III. *Happy single people tend to be gregarious loners.*

No matter how important your friends are, they will rarely be around as often as a spouse. So happy single people inevitably develop a liking for their own company. They become what I call gregarious loners—people who love having others around and love seeing them go.

What makes some men and women tolerate solitude so much better than others? Upbringing no doubt plays a role, because many of the happiest single people I know grew up as only children. They had no choice but to entertain themselves as youngsters and do the same quite nicely as adults.

People who lacked time alone in childhood often need to rediscover themselves as they grow older. Psychologists often urge them to do this through hobbies that can be pursued in solitude.

A better idea might be to think in terms of developing *interests* that can be enjoyed alone or with friends. Although I don't collect stamps or coins and will never do needlepoint, I have a lively interest in opera, theater, and ballet. I attend performances with friends and listen to musical scores when alone. What I get from cultural pursuits, others get from sports or politics.

Some activities offer so many rewards as to be worth investigating by almost everybody who is single. One is keeping a journal. Another is appreciating nature, whether by hiking in the woods or growing tomatoes on your terrace. A third is playing an instrument, especially if it is one that lends itself well to sharing with others. I have known single people whose lives were changed, quite dramatically, simply by learning to play the piano or the guitar. Their instrument didn't just give them a way to enrich any hours they spent alone; it also gave them a means of sharing their talents with their friends. And it boosted their self-confidence in a way that few other pursuits could have, because it brought them applause.

IV. *Happy single people rally round their rituals.*

A lot of single people I know don't miss being married so much as they miss participating in family rituals, like hauling home a Christmas tree or making root beer on July Fourth. And such traditions represent more than hollow observances.

Rituals matter partly because they make you feel connected to a group and, therefore, a little less alone. They also provide a channel through which people can express their deepest human emotions, including hope, joy, love,

and sorrow. Freud once noted that people who lack established rituals they can turn to in a crisis often invent their
own. And their inventions aren't necessarily beneficial.
Someone who doesn't attend a relative's funeral might
grieve instead by drinking heavily or by turning to drugs. A
person who doesn't celebrate a holiday might be ambushed
by depression a few weeks later when the reality of the loss
catches up.

New or old, the most satisfying rituals tend to involve
people you care about deeply. One man refused to give a
party in December, insisting he'd long since OD'd on his
friends' Christmas celebrations. He eventually decided to
give an annual beer and spaghetti supper in January,
sweeping in all of the friends he'd have otherwise seen
during the holidays. The event, he says now, draws nearly
one hundred percent attendance, because it competes with
few other diversions. Another always takes his niece and
nephew to see *The Nutcracker* at Lincoln Center, followed
by hot chocolate at Rumpelmayer's. And a third annually
buys a block of tickets for his high school homecoming
game, then invites his closest childhood friends to a tailgate
picnic in the parking lot before the gridiron action begins.

I try to strike a balance between rituals I observe mostly
for myself and traditions shared with friends. In the former
category, I buy white poinsettias at Christmas and lilies at
Easter. In the latter, I give an annual St. Patrick's Day get-
together, complete with a pot of Irish stew on the stove and
a Chieftains' album on the stereo. A Jewish friend affixes a
small mezuzah to the doorjamb of any apartment she lives
in and tries always to light candles at sundown on Friday,
even when it means having to tuck some into a duffel bag
before she heads for her ski house.

Such observances serve as touchstones that allow single
people to identify themselves by the customs they keep. Far
from the homes in which they grew up, unattached men
and women can reaffirm their past and anticipate the future
by giving concrete form to the values they hold dear.

V. *Happy single people live with their homes instead of merely in them.*

Your "home" doesn't have to be a house or even a fancy apartment. As T. S. Eliot said, "Home is where one starts from." If you are lucky, yours will welcome you each time you return to it.

The space you inhabit matters partly because it is one face that you present to the world. As such, it often says far more than you are willing to say about yourself. Your home is also the primary place where you connect with your family, honorary or otherwise. A home that you can live *with*, instead of merely *in*, makes it that much easier to be fully yourself.

Visiting the home of a happy single person, you feel that somebody has settled in, or at least stopped camping out. You see framed pictures on the walls, cozy pillows on the sofa, family photos on the shelf, and curtains on the windows. You also see lovingly tended plants or other evidence of flourishing life. One of the most attractive single men I know once won my heart with a tank of spectacular tropical fish, lit to glow in the dark. (Surely, I reasoned, anybody who tended his aquatic creatures so lovingly would be able to move up to higher orders, including single females.) Another man doomed his chances forever by leading me through his huge but barren penthouse overlooking a river. Not a print graced its walls or a rug its floors; there existed not even a well-thumbed *Forbes* casually tossed onto a coffee table. The austerity might have made sense had he been an impoverished artist or only just moved in. But his way of remaining in a state of suspended animation had been to coexist for years with what was really a high-priced cell. Why, I once asked, had he held his furnishings to a minimum? He replied that his first wife had gotten a lot of things in their divorce five years earlier, and he had never bothered to replace them because another woman was sure to come along soon, with tastes of her own.

Although even the smallest apartment can become a soothing decompression chamber, special graces flow from owning a home of your own. In observing single people, I have looked especially at those who have remained unmarried past thirty or become single late in life, through divorce or widowhood. Why, I asked, did some flourish while others dwindled with every year? One answer presented itself, time after time: the happy ones owned houses that took on personalities all their own. Often a house seemed to become a sort of surrogate spouse, storing memories and offering comfort, while giving its owner something to care for. It also became a still point helping to anchor a life against storms, and perhaps one of many such still points that provided continuity and stability.

For my widowed grandmother, home was a two-room shack, in the Pine Barrens of New Jersey, without running water or an indoor bathroom. But her husband had built it when he first came to this country, and she had tended it for thirty years. Day lilies grew up beside it, and honeysuckle vines climbed up its sides. Early on, she planted weeping willows that grew to tower above the roof. Inside, a spotless oilcloth covered the kitchen table, and a Sacred Heart picture had been tacked up over the bed. No home was more loved or provided more comforting continuity from one season to the next.

Lacking a home that shelters generations of memories, single men and women can still find ways to personalize the spaces they inhabit. A battered steamer trunk, from college, makes a far cheerier coffee table when topped with a wicker basket filled with burnished red apples. Snapshots culled from relatives can brighten a mantelpiece in need of refinishing. And an armload of wild flowers, from the backyard of a friend, can make an entire room sing.

VI. *Happy single people acquire cheerleading squads.*

Married people tend to assume that a single person's biggest problem is not having somebody around when things go wrong (the drain backs up, the job falls through, the neighborhood cat burglar pays a courtesy call on your apartment). But it can be worse not to have somebody around when things go *right* (the promotion arrives at last, the blind date "takes," the apartment looks sensational after a major redecoration). A lot of single people—and I am one of them—actually like to be alone when unhappy. A good, solitary cry can fix you up in no time. (Misery, in my book, does not love company so much as privacy.) Not many people like to be alone amid great joy, which always seems meant to be shared.

To share your own happiness, you need to find people who will care about your successes and delight in them with you. These people can turn up among friends your own age or in your profession. But both may need to be forgiven for their twinges of jealousy when you succeed where they haven't, or simply for lacking the perspective to recognize a triumph as such. Older friends or couples can often supply what peers can't.

VII. *Happy single people feel financially secure.*

If money can't buy you love, it can buy you peace of mind, particularly when you are single. Married people who fall short of cash often find themselves bailed out by their spouses. Single people need to bankroll themselves or risk having to turn to parents from whom they are trying to win independence.

More important than how much you earn is whether you feel your financial future is secure. I have known divorced multimillionaires who lived in perpetual dread of a downturn in the market—and unmarried novelists who made do quite cheerfully on unemployment checks and the belief that solvency was always just around the corner.

As a fledgling writer in her early twenties, I often felt poor, yet hopeful of eventual literary and financial redemption. So who cared about things like life insurance and Keogh Plans? As I have aged, my attitudes have changed, and what made me feel secure at twenty-two wouldn't have done the trick at thirty-two. You, too, need to keep revising your financial plan to reflect your changing needs.

VIII. *Happy single people find a way to nurture the next generation.*

Just as many single people lack friends of one sex or the other, so do they lack children. I moved out of Manhattan partly because, in the eight years I lived there as a single woman, I never lived in a building occupied by a minor. In the East Side high- and low-rises that I called home, no tricycles caromed off the walls and no "Sesame Street" songs echoed through the corridors. It wasn't that I was trying to avoid children, only that they are practically an endangered species in many large, expensive cities, including New York. (It seems that many married couples move out of the city after they have children and those who stay tend to pack their children off to boarding schools where they may make the acquaintance of fresh air and trees.) Then I moved to Boston and volunteered to teach Sunday school at a large urban church, only to be told it didn't *have* a Sunday school because it had too few children. It took several years of shopping around to find the church that needed me.

As a single adult, you *can* have children in your life, with benefits that aren't just social. The truth is that being unmarried is often a lot easier than not having children, because you can always get married. But you can't always have children who provide most people's best hope for ensuring that what they've learned will be passed on to others. These realities make it important for single people of any age to find ways to care for those who are younger, if only by a few years.

Many single men and women have begun to channel their nurturing instincts into mentoring. Most colleges have career-services departments, or even old-fashioned placement offices, that provide recent graduates with lists of older alums willing to offer advice. These services provide a wonderful way for new and old grads to find each other. Even if you've only been out of school a short time, you can share your experiences with someone who's never been out at all.

Other single people find younger friends by teaching night courses or taking on civic projects that attract a cross section of ages. And some, of course, seek out children directly, by teaching Sunday school or rediscovering younger relatives whom they scarcely knew in childhood.

IX. *Happy single people put down roots in a community.*

When you are very young it is entirely possible to live blissfully on the wing, never knowing where your mail will arrive from one week to the next. It's probably no accident that one of the most popular young adult magazines ever is called *Rolling Stone.* Sooner or later, though, most people want to put down roots in a community they can call home.

A major problem for single people is that they often live in large cities in which community is at a premium. The suburbs may not hold much appeal, and what else is there?

Many men and women find the answer in moving to a smaller city, as I did in leaving New York for the tamer shores of Boston. But so major an uprooting may not be required.

City neighborhoods often vary dramatically in the sense of community felt by their residents. One may offer little more than a place to drop anchor. Another may have a block association, community garden, sidewalk fair, and nighttime security patrols arranged by its residents. So you may need only to move across town to find yourself far happier with your life.

What unites people most effectively can vary widely among cities or neighborhoods. But it's almost always possible to link up with a Republican or Democratic committee that brings residents together for meetings and fund raisers.

Most cities also have chapters of community service organizations such as the Jaycees or Junior League. And no law says you can't go to school board meetings because you don't have a child or to zoning commission hearings because you don't own a house.

X. *Happy single people enjoy their work but don't sleep with their job descriptions.*

Hardly anybody needs to be reminded that being single, in the 1980s, can be a passport to professional superstardom. No longer is a spouse a virtual necessity for anyone who wants to scramble up a corporate ladder; today, a partner can even be a liability, especially when his or her career aims conflict with your own.

An unattached adult often succeeds at work partly because he or she has the time to give to it. One survey found that a typical top management executive spends fifty-five to sixty hours a week on the job, including work done at home. A single employee has those hours to give—and to give ungrudgingly. He or she does not have to weigh domestic concerns against professional obligations or to bushwhack a trail through a tangle of marital responsibilities in order to rise to the top of the corporate heap.

But the professional freedoms bring risks of their own. The most dangerous is that you'll wind up wedded to your work—or at least sleeping with your job description. A lot of single people work exorbitantly long hours, at the beginning of their careers, in order to prove themselves to their bosses. But they continue to drive themselves mercilessly long after they've earned a little relaxation, because they never learned how to put on the brakes. They often spend too much time relating to products and not enough relating to people, allowing work to squeeze out anything but one-night stands or casual romances that scarcely last from one weekend to the next.

Even so, workaholism can be easy to cure when you are single. A married man or woman might be tempted to jus-

tify staying on a treadmill to provide for a growing family.
It's a rare single person who can't get off if he or she wants
to. What it takes to do it is mostly a little planning: for
vacations, out-of-town weekends, or just overdue nights on
the town.

Anchorwoman Diane Sawyer, who has remained unmarried into her late thirties, has said that she regularly recov-
ers from a strenuous week in front of the cameras by going
to as many as three movies in succession after work on
Friday. More single people need to equip their lives with
such enforced R and Rs.

XI. *Happy single people have social lives that exist
     independently of their love lives.*

Few single people live in a more unhappy limbo than do
those who stay in lame-duck romances without which they
might have no social life at all. Many spend months or even
years in love affairs that have little to do with love, hoping
that marriage will someday redeem all their suffering.

One woman dates married men almost exclusively, even
though most admit up front that they will never leave their
wives. She says she does so because married men are the
only ones around and she doesn't want to "be alone." Paradoxically, however, her affairs keep her from developing
the sort of full and engaging social life that would allow her
to break free of them.

Single women, of course, have no monopoly on destructive romances. One young male doctor insists he's unhappy
dating only nurses and wants to get to know others. But he
has also convinced himself that only hospital personnel can
understand what his life is "really" like. Besides, he adds, he
has no way to meet others, when he's on call every third
night. He steadfastly refuses to take out a personals ad even
though the classifieds would allow him to specify the kind of
women he *would* like to meet and also to explain his limited
availability.

Happy single people, by contrast, go out mostly with people who are good to them and for them. They have that luxury partly because they know their engagement calendars will be full, whether they are seeing someone or not. They also tend to see their romances, not as ends in themselves, but merely as a means to greater happiness than they would have without them. Why be miserable with a date when you could be happy by yourself or with good friends?

It isn't always easy to break free of a single destructive romance, let alone a string of them. But that freedom always begins with the understanding that any love affair ought to raise you to a higher power—to bring out your strengths instead of your weaknesses. If a romance makes even *you* lose a little respect for you, it's time to move on.

XII. *Happy single people treat themselves as kindly as they would want a spouse to.*

Many single people who long desperately to take care of someone else have proved, nevertheless, to be barely adequate at taking care of themselves. They live on fast food, don't exercise much, and unwind after a workday by finishing off a bottle of wine instead of by talking to a friend. They do all these things partly because they believe they are only doing them temporarily. One day, they feel sure, they will get married and enjoy meals eaten sitting down at a table, instead of standing up in front of the refrigerator.

Happy single people, by contrast, treat themselves as kindly as they would if they were married. They do not cringe when told that "the mark of a civilized person is how you eat when you are alone," immediately envisioning themselves in a bearskin and a club. They may eat out a lot and eat frozen food, too. Still, they usually consume at least one hot, balanced meal a day. They do not subsist exclusively on yogurt or barbecued chicken, or even cold chicken noodle soup, forked straight out of the can. Their nutritional alphabet runs, if not from A to Z, at least not from A to C.

Happy single people take care of themselves in other ways, too. They don't, for instance, play the silent martyr in illness. They call a friend to ask for a quart of orange juice or a ride to the doctor's. They may not be able to make themselves better, but they don't use their marital status as an excuse to make themselves worse.

Taking care of yourself ultimately does more than help to keep you healthy. It also helps to keep you physically and mentally attractive to others. How you treat yourself is always an index to your self-respect. It says that *you* think you are important enough to cherish, whether or not somebody else does, and, often as not, that positive message isn't lost on the people you care most about.

XIII. *Happy single people live as though they could marry tomorrow but might remain single forever.*

Getting married, especially if you expect to have children, forces you to plan ahead. Nobody can put off forever deciding where to send the children to school or whether to go to Disneyland before they grow up. Neither can two people become parents without hoping for the best. So having a child is nothing if not an optimistic act—a leap of faith into a future that is believed to be good.

Without so tangible a reason to believe in the best that lies ahead, single people need to give themselves other reasons to look forward to tomorrow and beyond. They need to set long- and short-term goals and especially to seek new challenges to meet throughout a lifetime.

An act as simple as planning to take one great vacation a year often can add color to the entire rest of your life. It can also insure that you will never lack for something to look forward to. One of my aunts lost her father and brothers before she reached her twenties. Then she became a childless widow when her husband was killed on Guam. She had a secure though not glamorous job and an elderly mother to care for. Others might have viewed her life as cheerless, but she never did. One reason was that she was always looking forward to her next trip to Florida, a destination she once drove to in an old Packard with a running board. Sometimes she went to Florida with a man, other times with a female friend, and occasionally with her mother. What matters is that she went, and with a regularity that always gave her something happy to look ahead to.

My younger friends achieve a similar effect by planning annual trips to Europe or Nantucket. One woman savors her annual trip to France on more levels than one. Throughout the year she cooks dishes that she tried for the first time in Provence and she keeps her accent sharp with the help of language classes at the Alliance Française. One day she may grow tired of the destination that charms her today. I am convinced, however, that she will never grow tired of life, because a new destination will await her.

It almost doesn't matter what goals you set, so long as they reflect the reality that, though you could marry tomorrow, you might also be single forever. One single man decided, a few years ago, to see if he could reach the upper rungs of the squash ladder at his racquet club. This self-imposed challenge has long since given him more than a way to stay in shape. It has enhanced his vitality and his pride in his ability to achieve what he wants to, not just on the courts but in other places, too. Not the least of its benefits is that it has also given him new friends, because his increasing skill has required that he seek out new partners.

It especially matters that you try to do things you couldn't or wouldn't do if you were married—to take advantage of opportunities you may never have again. The trick is to exploit the unique advantages of singlehood that unhappy people merely try to escape.

I try, in planning my days, to avoid looking just to the moment, when there are always bookshelves to be dusted or the Sunday paper to be read. I mentally project forward a year and then ask, not what I would like to do in the intervening months, but what I would like to *have done* by the time they have ended. On December 31, I make a list not of

things to do in the coming year but of all the new things I
did for the first time during the one that has just passed. I list
the new friends made, the new places visited, and the new
activities tried. This way I gain a fix, not on where I want to
go, but on where I have been, a more accurate way to stay
in touch with whether I am moving forward socially, emotionally, financially, and professionally. Without such a list, I
might always be planning to live without ever getting
around to it.

Happy single people's lives don't have to include all of the
above, but they usually include a majority of them. Neither
does the absence of several mean you are fated to suffer.
Some men and women almost instinctively know how to
get what they want from life. The rest of us will always need
to work up to it. What matters is that you start somewhere
to move in the direction you want.

Wherever you are now, you can live for today—and also
for tomorrow. And the most direct route to doing that often
begins where you did: in a family.

3

Family of One

A few years ago, before I moved from New York to Boston, I took elaborate pains to insure a smooth transition from one home to the next. I lined up a terrific job in a field I knew well. I mastered Boston's public transportation system and checked out its libraries. I learned to say "rotary" instead of "traffic circle" and "dark rye" instead of "pumpernickel." I even selected charming temporary quarters, in an ivy-clad Tudor guesthouse, to insure that I wouldn't feel pressured into taking a less than dream apartment.

As my moving day approached, I had another cause for optimism. I had always been outgoing and seemed to make friends almost reflexively. Eight years earlier, when I landed in New York, I had found a close friend within three weeks and several more within six months. And those didn't even count all the dates and colleagues who rounded out my life. In Boston, I assumed, it would be no harder to connect with others.

What I hadn't taken into account was the role that serendipity had played in the friendships I'd acquired in the past.

At twenty-one, I had been surrounded by people who were single and had lots of time for friendship. Almost none had children who limited their availability. I was also living in a city only an hour from where I grew up and therefore remained close to many of my childhood friends. And I worked in magazine publishing, which attracted thousands of kindred spirits to the city I called home.

All that changed abruptly once I moved to Boston, where I became an instant outsider on more levels than one. It took nearly a year in my new home before I recognized the truth: no longer could I take for granted that compatible companions would turn up. I would have to *work* at making friends. It seemed inconceivable that any would one day form the sort of "extended family" I had known before. After a year at my new address, I would have been grateful just for someone who knew my Zip Code, let alone my darkest fears and secret aspirations.

Eventually I made friends, but not without learning some lessons, one of which stood out. Friendship, when you are single, is like money in the bank. You never really *know* how much you will need in a crisis. So it's best to store up more than you think you'd have to draw upon in a crunch.

How many friends are "enough"? Simone de Beauvoir once remarked that she has never felt lonely, because she knows she has enough friends so that, if several of them were killed at once in a car crash, she would still have others. That standard makes good sense and it's not surprising that it came from someone who has never married.

Yet De Beauvoir's guideline does not go quite far enough for many single people. Most of us need more than a critical mass of friends; we need to have it nearby. And this reality means that we may need more than one such group to sustain us in our different homes. I felt emotionally isolated in Boston not because I lacked enough friends to weather the sort of car crash De Beauvoir had envisioned. I felt alone because the ones I had were hundreds of miles away, and too often a WATS line didn't do enough to bridge the gap.

Like many single people, I had also failed to appreciate the difference between a friend and a colleague or to realize that I needed both. Even after I began to enjoy the company of many sympathetic companions, I still had too many prospective friends and too few colleagues, simply because Boston was home to far fewer magazines than was New York. I therefore had access to far fewer people who'd worked for the same kinds of publications I had and who spoke its specialized language.

The New Dowry: Friends

Other single people seem to have the opposite problem. Professional men and women often don't have friends so much as contacts or business associates. The differences may not become clear until you develop a personal problem of the sort better left out of the office. You need to talk to someone, but whom can you trust not to spill your confidences over the coffee wagon?

Insuring that you have both friends and colleagues begins with remembering that the former almost always come regularly to your home. A contact or business associate, by contrast, generally sees you in a professional setting. The gap can sometimes be bridged by inviting your coworkers home for drinks or dinner parties that give a boost to friendships in the wings. Yet you will always have things you won't want to discuss with anyone who might someday be in a position to use them against you. This fact makes it important that you always have friends from somewhere besides the office.

Another element comes into play as you move beyond your twenties into your thirties and especially your forties. It is what Dr. Srully Blotnick calls the crucial "pyramid factor" that emerges as people move up the corporate ladder. In his survey of business-career crises, *The Corporate*

Steeplechase (Facts on File, 1984), Blotnick notes that most people in their twenties work alongside many others doing a similar sort of work. As people gain more responsibility, the ranks of their peers thin out, until they have all but disappeared. Much further up the corporate ladder than they were earlier in their careers, men and women are left not with peers but subordinates, who generally make poor prospects for friendship.

Blotnick's survey only strengthens the case for having a rich and diverse circle of friends. At best this sphere will include not just men and women but people who are young and old, black and white, married and single. Having representatives of all these groups in your life will only enrich it if or when you marry. The Canadian journalist Merle Shain once said that if she were to remarry tomorrow she would take all her friends along with her as a sort of dowry. Then she would tell her new husband that he was getting a rich woman. The actress Candice Bergen, who married for the first time in her thirties, said in her autobiography, *Knock Wood* (Linden Press/Simon & Schuster, 1984), that she viewed her own friends as just such a "dowry."

The thorniest question single people face is how to amass that sort of human support system in cities in which they know almost no one but people with whom they share an office. All too often, it can take years to put such a group together, and meanwhile you may find yourself scrounging for every crust of friendship you can get.

Common interests and values beget friendships, but they alone are rarely enough to give rise to deep bonds. To forge those ties you also need to spend ample time with kindred spirits. Unattached men and women often lament that they aren't developing close friendships even though they are doing what they believe to be the "right" thing, such as going out for lunch or drinks with people they'd like to know better. They usually *are* doing the right thing, but just not enough of it. It can take months or even years of meeting for occasional meals or drinks for a new friendship to take root. When too much time elapses between meetings, you tend to spend all of your time catching up on what has happened, without ever getting around to what it all really meant.

All of this helps to explain why it's almost never a bad idea to try to meet regularly with someone to whom you are or would like to be close. I am grateful to a friend who suggested, as our respective schedules grew progressively more complicated, that we try to meet for lunch once a month on the same day, so we would never go too long without seeing each other. The busier you are the harder you may need to try to find a way to institutionalize your meetings. Edward I. Koch, the unmarried mayor of New York, has lunch at least three times a week with his close friend Dan Wolf, the founding editor of the *Village Voice*. Sometimes, the mayor has said, they have lunch as much as five times a week, and always at the same place, to reduce scheduling problems. More single people need to follow his lead, to insure that they'll share as much with friends as others would with their spouses. It's also a good idea to try to call at least one friend every day for the same sort of social chat you'd have nightly with a spouse.

Regular conversations with friends especially help to insure that you'll discuss the little things that matter to you along with the big ones. Many single people fear that they will have no one with whom to share the really important events of their lives, a worry that frequently proves unfounded. Friends rally round you very quickly when something big happens, partly because the news of it tends to travel quickly. Friends may not rally round you when something smaller occurs, largely because the news of it may not spread at all. I rarely call or visit someone else simply to say I've bought a new Linda Rondstadt album, seen the tulips in the Public Garden, or finished reading another chapter of a moving book, though I would share such things with a spouse. Instead I make an effort to see my friends a lot, so that such matters can come up naturally in the course of our discussion.

Shortcuts to Sharing

But what if you don't have anyone at all with whom to share such things, or at least have them nearby? Then you need to try to find ways to compress the time it takes to get to know other people, something you can accomplish in more than several ways.

One is to pursue people likely to be more open to friendship than others. These include people who have just moved to town or into your building. To forge some sort of connection, you often need do nothing more than offer a little help. Volunteer to show someone around or to provide the names of trusted professionals such as doctors and mechanics who work wonders with Honda Accords.

Be sensitive, in any case, to matters of personal timing. Someone I liked a lot once tried to meet me for lunch at a time when my nonstop job left little time for socializing. Graciously, she didn't press me to schedule get-togethers I didn't have room for. After hearing that I'd left the job, she called me again, and our friendship flowered under more favorable conditions.

Another way to reduce the time it takes to make a new friend is to take up activities that allow you to spend entire weekends with people with similar interests. Over a two- or three-day period, you may be able to spend as much time with someone as you would in months of after-work drinks. Apart from their job-related benefits, professional conferences and seminars can leave you with lots of prospective friends. So can church retreats or weekend outings sponsored by social clubs. Sporting organizations tend especially to give single people terrific opportunities to connect not just for one weekend but many. Going to your college reunion every year, instead of once a decade, can also lead to friendships. So can a fast trip to a nearby Club Med, which offers weekend packages as well as longer ones.

Another way to telescope the process of making new acquaintances is to do something ritualistically a couple of times a week. It can be hard to reach out to somebody you've met only once or twice, no matter how good the vibes between the two of you seem to be. The more you connect the easier it gets, and the more likely you will be to choose the right person to go after. So regular jazz dance classes can be as good for your social calendar as they are for your cardiovascular system. And you can scarcely help but make new friends when you take up activities that require you to find partners or work in concert with others: folk dancing, racquetball, acting with an amateur theater troupe, or volunteering two Saturdays a month at a re-cycling center or crisis hot line. I met one of my closest friends while working without pay on a low-budget cable TV show produced by a social club for young, professional New Yorkers. An instant bond emerged the night a guest herpetologist appeared on the set, bringing a boa constric-tor with him, and the two of us simultaneously turned around and sought safety in another part of the studio. As I have become better established professionally, I've also made close friends through serving on boards of civic as-sociations and nonprofit institutions. It almost doesn't mat-ter what activity you choose so long as you love it and share it often with others.

But can't you count on making a lot of friends just by being neighborly to your neighbors? Of course. But in the years I've been single I've never made a close friend of someone who lived in the next apartment, or even on my floor—and my experience is far from unique. It probably represents, in fact, the rule rather than the exception. It seems that, while most single people would like the benefits of having a close friend nearby, they also fear a possible erosion of privacy. The idea apparently is that, if you make a friend on your floor, you might well have someone whose buzzer you can ring when you hear a prowler on the fire escape and want to call a cop. At the same time, you never can tell when the same person might appear at your door, asking to borrow a tray of ice cubes, just when you have smeared your entire face with an oatmeal-almond masque or are in the middle of trying to bench-press four hundred fifty pounds.

Similarly, few single people can count on becoming very close to their roommates. A dear friend, by definition, is someone who is always "there" for you. But what most single people want in a roommate is frankly someone who is not there: a man or woman who spends a lot of time on the road, or at someone else's place. Most apartments simply are not big enough to shelter two discrete personalities for long. A biological sink comes into being as its tenants begin to knock heads, no matter how much they like each other. So the most successful roommate arrangements tend to be those in which two or more people actually try to *keep* some distance between them, precisely the opposite of what most single people want to do with their friends.

Not all proximity, however, begets tension as surely as it does clutter. A lot of single people live together, not full time, but on an off-again, on-again basis in weekend beach or ski houses. These part-time communal households can provide a perfect culture medium for friendship. Most people spend long enough in them to have a real chance to get to know others, but not so long that they feel trapped. Many of my fondest memories were made at a beach house in the Hamptons, complete with a barbecue grill and tennis court that helped bring people together. How could I not enjoy spending six weekends a summer in a sprawling house with a dozen or so others when the rest of the time I spent rattling around in a one-room apartment by myself?

Many large cities enable single people to rent houses together year round, an especially good idea for people who are just moving to an area. You don't feel so cooped up in a big house as you do in an apartment, and houses can often be cheaper, too. Some group residences aim to bring together single people of a particular persuasion, such as non-smokers or vegetarians, thereby helping to insure that all tenants will have at least something in common. I left Manhattan partly because such houses were nowhere to be found on an island comprised of almost no single- or double-family houses suitable for rental to a group. In my adopted city, they thrive, thanks partly to papers such as the Boston *Phoenix*, in which people advertise regularly for house-mates.

Though I've never lived in a communal household, it is a blessing to know I could, should solitary living begin to chafe. Other single people find community in the new "mingles" condos gaining popularity around the country. They're not much different from most other forms of housing, except that they have extra bathrooms, so that each occupant can have a private one. A one-bedroom mingles condo, for instance, might have two bathrooms instead of the usual one. These and similar ways of finding companionship can make being single a lot more fun.

A Job Description for Friendship

Even time and proximity in ample doses, though, may not be enough to spawn honorary families. To make friends, you've got to be one to others, often in ways you couldn't have expected. It might have been easy enough to make friends with someone who sat next to you in Psych 101, when all you had to do was make a copy of the class notes you took when he or she was sick. The responsibilities—not to mention the rewards—of adult friendship can be far more complex. And they inevitably involve taking risks that may feel uncomfortable at first.

Foremost among the things that adult friends need to do for each other is simply to keep their state secrets, whether or not they've been asked. One of the great appeals of marriage is that at least theoretically it gives men and women the knowledge that their deepest confidences are safe with at least one other person. So single men and women can—and need to—provide the same service for each other. Nobody should ever need to *ask* you not to repeat what you've been told about his or her sex life, job search, or bank book. I tell my troubles to my friend Susan Samuelson, not just because she is a sensitive listener, but because I know she would not violate my confidences should the KGB show up at her door with chains and billy clubs. Before you are tempted to repeat what someone told you the other day at the racquetball club, ask whether you would disclose the same information had it been given to you by a spouse.

The second thing friends owe each other is another form of loyalty. The people you're close to ought to be able to assume that you'll never criticize them in public, whether or not they are around to hear it. I would go one step further and say that you also shouldn't criticize a friend in private, even if he or she has asked for it. The truth is that what a friend asks for isn't always what he or she wants or needs. And giving even the gentlest criticism can imperil your relations gravely. I once poured out to a friend a list of painful experiences that had left me emotionally flattened. It was hard to see, I said, what benefit could result from facing so many tragedies within so short a time. Attempting to offer consolation, the woman volunteered that she'd often found it hard to talk to me in the past, but that she didn't anymore because my problems were forcing me to "open up," thereby strengthening our friendship. Instead of providing comfort, her comment only made me feel worse. It simply gave me one more worry: that people might perceive me as aloof. I also felt angry at the implication that tragedies of the magnitude I'd been discussing could possibly be redeemed by the knowledge that our friendship had grown stronger as a result. What *would* have strengthened our friendship was simply a little praise that might have helped me over my hurdles. If she couldn't have said truthfully that she admired my handling of my present troubles, she might have recalled how well I'd handled another problem in the past and expressed confidence that the qualities I'd displayed then would come to my aid again.

Anything that might be interpreted as criticism of a friend is best phrased in terms of a question from which others can draw their own conclusions. One single woman asked a man she liked a lot for an appraisal of the decor in her small but charming apartment. Believing she wanted frankness, he scarcely thought before he replied: "It's lovely, except for that ratty old armoire, which you ought to send to the dumpster." The piece had belonged to the woman's favorite grandmother and was the one possession she never wanted to part with. Her friend needn't have lied and said he loved it when he didn't. But neither should he have deluded himself into thinking that his initial praise would have taken the sting out of an attack on one of her favorite objects. A kinder answer might have been to suggest moving the armoire to a different location or painting it a different color. Better still would have been to ask a question that would have elicited her feelings about the object before he tore into it. ("Have you ever considered getting the armoire refinished by that great antiques restorer who did Kevin's library table?") Most single people get all the criticism they need from their parents, relatives, and employers. To add more, even inadvertently, is simply to miss the point of what friendship is all about, which is to make others feel unconditionally accepted and valued.

Just as friends have an obligation to withhold gratuitous criticism, they also need to offer liberal doses of praise. You almost can't get too excited about someone's new project, apartment, or outfit. Good friends are always trying to make you feel uniquely interesting and appreciated. They praise not just what you do or wear but also what you *are*. One woman always seems to be starting sentences by saying, "It means so much to me that you . . . ," "You have helped me

so much by . . . ," or "One of the wonderful things about
you is . . ." A man once wrote to me, after I'd spent hours
discussing his career plans, "I'm not sure what I'm going to
do, but I just wanted to let you know how glad I am to have
you nearby and to know I can call you when I need to."
Especially if your life doesn't have as many friends as you'd
hoped, try to get into the habit of paying at least three or
four compliments a day to people you'd like to know better
and several more to the men and women you are already
crazy about.

To praise others often, you've got to pay minute attention
to the details of what they say and do. Just as you can't give
your friends too much praise, you also can't have too good a
memory for what someone told you last time and needs to
be asked about this time. It's appalling what some people
forget to ask about, such as how your annual review went on
Friday or whether the lab test showed you really did get
malaria from the mosquito that bit you in Haiti. A good
friend instantly notices when you're wearing something
new, have moved a picture in the hall, or have managed to
pull off a remarkable achievement at work. He or she re-
members, when you've just gotten a raise, that it was actually your second this year, and makes sure that the other
guests at a dinner party know that you won a local road race
last Saturday.

A good friend notices, in short, what other people
couldn't or *wouldn't*, and lets you know that he or she has.
One of the most beloved women I know has made a small
specialty of remembering precisely what people have told
her from one meeting to the next. Her memory is so accurate that some of her friends swear she has to take notes
when they're not looking. I recently watched the woman at
work at a dinner party involving several of her closest
friends. Taking one man by the arm, she steered him gently
toward another. "Oh, you've got to meet Stan," she said, full
of enthusiasm. "He always says, as you do, how much he
actually *prefers* Los Angeles to San Francisco." Then she

ran into a lawyer whom she hadn't seen in months. "It's so great to see you," she said instantly. "I was just wondering yesterday how things were going on the antitrust case you told me about at the Smiths'." The overall effect, to anyone who watched her, was really quite remarkable, yet not at all insincere. She made all the people she spoke to feel important and appreciated, largely because they were.

Part of praising your friends is praising *their* friends, or at least not criticizing them, either in public or in private. At least two benefits result from withholding uncharitable remarks. The first is that you avoid wounding a person who means a lot to you. People choose their friends as surely as they select anything else, and to impugn them is to question their taste. The second benefit of not maligning your friends' friends—and indeed of making every possible effort to praise them—is that it keeps your credit rating clean. I never listen to a friend light into a mutual acquaintance without wondering whether I will someday suffer the same fate. I wonder the same thing when I listen to someone else repeat gossip that, though not necessarily unflattering, might be better left unsaid. Neither of these inevitably causes me to stop seeing someone, but it can cause me to express my thoughts and feelings less openly. This, in turn, can keep our friendship superficial instead of allowing it to go deeper.

Yet it would be a mistake to suggest that friends merely offer each other intangibles, such as words of uplift and encouragement, however vital they are. Good friends also do concrete things for each other, of which the following are some:

• *They fuss over their friends' hurts.* The hardest part about getting sick when you are single may not be the illness itself. It can instead be the lack of someone to take care of you. Good friends almost always have at least one unofficial nurse or doctor on twenty-four hour call, because they are always taking care of others who happily return the favor. One single man has for weeks been driving an injured fellow skier to his regular physical therapy sessions. A woman jots down in her engagement calendar the days of her friends' doctors' appointments and calls an hour or so afterward to find out how they went.

At times, you may need to be a little cheeky to make sure your offers to help are accepted. Nobody really likes to admit weakness or vulnerability, and single people are especially likely to feel they ought to be able to do everything on their own. So your offers of assistance may meet with initial resistance, which you'll need to look beyond. Leave a container of take-out won-ton soup, which you have labeled "Chinese Chicken Soup," with the doorman of a bedridden friend (who nonetheless insists he needs "nothing"). With it include the day's *Wall Street Journal* and maybe the new *Esquire*. Take a bouquet of anemones to someone laid up with bronchitis.

• *They help each other move.* Perhaps the only thing that can feel worse than being sick when you are single is moving when you are single. A move, however much you look forward to it, always represents a kind of death—the ending of one phase of life and the beginning of another. So, no less than when someone dies in the family of a friend, you need to find something you can do to ease the pain. Help pack, if you can. Make another gesture, if you can't. I needed to do very little packing when I left Manhattan because I had sublet my apartment fully furnished. I had also planned to move on a weekday morning when most of my friends would be at work. My friend Amy Greenhill nonetheless came up to my apartment at 7:30 A.M., before she went to her office, with warm blueberry muffins that we could share during my last few hours in town. Another woman called me at 5:05 P.M., on my first day in my new job, to ask how it had gone and to ask about my new home. Other acquaintances arranged so many going-away parties that I felt like a Southern debutante in reverse; I wasn't having a cycle of coming-out parties, I was having a flurry of going-out ones. But perhaps no one helped more than my friend Rick Hampson, who drove to New York from Springfield, Massachusetts, to drive me to Boston with my belongings packed into his trunk. His assistance allowed me to avoid the moments I most dreaded: waving good-bye, all alone, to my friends in New York, and arriving, all alone, at my new home in Boston. All the help touched me greatly and turned what could have been a trauma into a warm and happy rite of passage.

• *They honor their friends' big days.* Nothing cements a friendship so solidly as sharing a landmark event together, whether it's a housewarming or a family funeral. When you participate in some event that someone else will remember for a lifetime, you become part of a memory that can raise your relations to a new level. Your simply being there says you care in a way that you might not otherwise have been able to express. To paraphrase Woody Allen, eighty percent of friendship is just showing up. So it makes sense to try to attend as many of your friends' special events as you can. Be there for their showers, their weddings, and their children's christenings. Attend the meetings where they're giving speeches and the dinners where they're getting awards. And be sure that, when something big happens to you, your friends hear the news directly from you. Allow your important news to reach them second or third hand, and they may justifiably wonder whether you care less about them than about somebody else.

Many single people reliably attend their friends' five-star events, such as their bridal showers or bachelor parties. The same men and women have far less impressive records when it comes to putting in appearances at two-star occasions, such as dinner parties or Sunday brunches. This negligence can be fatal to a friendship. A friend's annual Christmas gala might be one of thirteen to which you have received invitations, including two others for the same night. But that doesn't mean your acquaintance doesn't need you there or won't notice if you aren't.

I have recently been trying to devise a sort of litmus test for friendship—to name the one thing that separates the people who are your friends from those who aren't. The best I have been able to come up with is simply this: a good friend is somebody you know will attend your party unless he or she is either (a) in traction or (b) on assignment with Dan Rather in El Salvador. Good friends are not forever begging out of your dinner parties on the grounds that they have to work late, can't get a baby-sitter, or are "incredibly busy" these days. Should you ever find yourself in the position of having to offer such an excuse, at least try to send flowers on the day of the event or to make another tangible gesture to prove you are there in spirit.

• *They touch each other frequently.* So much hugging and kissing goes on among my closest companions that I sometimes wonder whether it is possible to reach out and touch someone too often. But you can't. As research increasingly shows, frequent demonstrations of affection represent far more than meaningless games of kissy-face. Dr. James Lynch reported in *The Broken Heart: The Medical Consequences of Loneliness* (Basic Books, 1977) that the human touch can have psychological as well as physical benefits that deserve further study.

Psychologists use the term "skin hunger" to describe the sense of loss many people feel when they go too long without being touched by somebody else. It is a feeling that most single people know well. One single woman says, only half jokingly, that she has sometimes considered making an appointment to get her hair shampooed and blown dry just to be touched by somebody else.

A single person's need to be touched can often be satisfied quite nicely by a pat on the arm or back. I make it a point always to shake hands with others, not just when we greet each other, but also when we are leaving. Close friends get not just handshakes but hugs, kisses, and other forms of touching. I once gave manicures and daily foot massages to a friend in the hospital—a practice doctors said could also help to improve circulation.

• *They return each other's phone calls instantly.* The members of loving families do not wait three days to return each other's phone calls simply because it is more convenient—they get back to each other as soon as possible. And good *friends* don't delay either. The day may come soon enough when you will face a big or little crisis and need to talk to somebody about it immediately. In order to be sure you will be able to reach the friends who can help, you've got to make a habit of being there for *them* now.

It's also essential to have good telephone manners. Begin every phone conversation by asking whether it's a good time to talk. And try to end every conversation by recalling in positive terms something said during it, as you might by saying: "Your new apartment sounds wonderful, and I'll think of you warming yourself in front of your fireplace."

Similarly, good friends respond quickly to your letters and cards. It seems they are always dashing off little notes to let you know how much they appreciate something you have done. Not long ago, after I read in the papers that a prominent television personality had died, I quickly wrote a friend who'd been close to her. Almost immediately I received back the following note:

Dear Jan,
Your note had a very special meaning for me at a very trying time. Thanks for being there.
Fondly,
Mike.

A mere two sentences let me know that my friend had received my note and helped to shore up a friendship both of us value. If you find it hard to express your deepest feelings—either over the telephone or on paper—make a habit of stockpiling cards that you can send when the need arises.

• *They give each other shelter.* Robert Frost once remarked that home is where, when you go there, they've got to take you in. Good friends are people who *want* to take you in. In fact, if I were asked to name the most important thing people could do to make more and closer friends, I would say simply this: have an open-door policy. Let all of your friends or prospective friends know they are welcome to stay at your place as often as they want for as long as they can. Good friends never abuse such privileges and are, anyway, really giving you the privilege of their company.

Allowing people to stay with you can probably do more than anything else to help you make friends quickly, partly because it provides the time and proximity to someone else that friendship requires. Besides, your home says more about you than almost anything else and gives other people a chance to respond to it. So, unless you have a roommate whose privacy has to be respected, you almost can't have people over too much. Rarely will others object to less than swank accommodations. Even when I lived in apartments so small it was scarcely possible to exhale in them without hitting a wall, I still offered others a chance to spend the night in a sleeping bag on the floor. City hotel prices being what they are, the offer was usually accepted. In my summer cottage I have two nylon L. L. Bean cots that are more comfortable than many convertible sofas. They can also be folded up to fit in a closet. They are so practical that I may buy a few more to accommodate guests in my city apartment.

• *They give each other gifts.* Single people who don't have children need to make a special effort to insure that they will give to others as much as parents do to their offspring. On one level, they can offer intangibles, such as praise and support. On another, they can give real gifts— not just holiday and birthday presents but year-round ones, too. Ultimately, such tributes are among the spores that single people send out into the world where they may root and flower. Presents also show your friends that you appreciate their own uniqueness. Once you have reached adulthood, without getting married, you can go for years without getting a present that is exactly what you had your heart set on—the big or little equivalent of your own red pony, in Steinbeck's story of the same name. Parents and relatives can lose touch with what you are all about, and lovers' gifts can reflect an agenda more theirs than your own. But you can give your friends what their kin may not. If you can't give the sort of big, expensive gifts that a spouse might, you can do something just as important by giving smaller ones more often. Make a point of stocking up on these all year round so that you are never caught shorthanded when an occasion rolls around.

Developing a sort of specialty can help a lot, too. I have for many years maintained a manila folder of cartoons from *The New Yorker* and the old *Saturday Review*, where I once worked. I especially save drawings that pertain to the occupations of my friends and then get them framed as a holiday or birthday nears. (Some cartoons I have kept for years, knowing that I will someday have a friend who will appreciate them.) A woman I know roots cuttings from her grape ivy plants that she is always giving out in ceramic pots. My friend Bud uses his carpenter's lathe to turn out bookends and wood coasters for friends. Another acquaintance takes photos of her friends with her Nikon, then gets them framed and gives them out at Christmas. You might take small presents, not bottles of wine, to dinner parties and weekends in the country.

Giving presents to married friends as well as single ones turns out to be less a duty than a privilege. All too often, single people think that their married friends' spouses meet all their needs, including their need to have their importance acknowledged by a tangible gift. In reality, what a husband gives his wife is often as prosaic as a six-slice toaster

—and what she gives to him is the color shirt that he hates but that she thinks he will look good in. At holidays or any other time, single people can often become the leaven that causes somebody else's life to rise, where it might once have lain flat.

Doing all—or any—of these things never guarantees that you will have friends, let alone an honorary family, nearly so soon as you'd like. Yet it's a rare man or woman who could do all without making a few. If you are lucky, you will simply make several close friends a year, or even one or two, until you arrive at a point at which you feel as rich as a Rothschild in the affection of others. Hope chests have gone out of fashion, but you can still have a dowry that only increases in value. And, best of all, you don't have to marry to share it with someone else.

4

Dates for Straights

Every few years or so, the newspapers publish a story about someone who grew so desperate to find love that he or she decided to advertise for it on a billboard. When I lived in Manhattan, the papers there reported that one man grew so tired of sitting home alone that he put up a sign in Grand Central Station, on which he requested letters from eligible women. The news media later reported that he had been swamped with offers but still hadn't found the woman of his dreams. More recently, a wire service dispatch told of a Texas man who posted a sign reading: WIFE WANTED, NEW OR USED, KIDS O.K. The story said that thirty women responded, but the closest the man got to eternal love was a three-day courtship of a woman who dropped him because, she said, he was "too pushy."

As much as I have occasionally longed for someone to share my pillow or my *Playbill,* I have to admit that I have never grown desperate enough to advertise my plight on a billboard. But I know exactly how the people who take such reckless measures feel, because I've been there in spirit. So have many of my friends.

As the poets have always said, the course of true love never runs smoothly. What the poets have not said is that sometimes the course of true love does not run at all, and what's a body to do then?

One thing is clear: no matter how hard you try, you can't will yourself to fall in love. You can't even force yourself to find someone with whom you could. The best you can do in most cases is to try to set the stage for romance, so that you will have created a space for it in your life, if or when it happens to be in the cards for you.

Setting Love's Stage

The *good* news is that there are more ways than ever to set that stage successfully. They range from time-honored practices that might be looked at afresh to more recent inventions that many single people have yet to catch up with.

The most obvious thing you can do to give your love life a boost is simply to consider packaging yourself a little differently. I had to have been crazy not to get contact lenses until I reached twenty-nine. I had to have been even crazier not to have gotten an expert's advice on choosing the right eyeglass frames for my face for as long as I wore them. It's not that I lacked for dates during the time I didn't do either; it's just that I will never know how many more I might have had otherwise. I know a man whose love life turned a corner after he visited a branch office of the Diet Center, which helped him lose thirty pounds.

A female friend's love life revved up after she engaged the services of a personal shopper at a large department store. It seems that the woman, a stockbroker, had always believed that her profession required her to dress in drab blues and grays that seemed to drag her personality down; a fashion consultant showed her how to add a little color to her wardrobe and thereby to her life. Her new clothes caused her to be noticed for the first time by a vice-president of her company, to whom she is now engaged.

Most of us can't count on our friends to provide objective advice on such matters, because they'd love us in sackcloth. So an expert's opinion can often be what makes the central difference in boosting your candlepower with the other sex.

Another way to punch up your love life is to move to a new neighborhood or, if it was in the cards anyway, to change jobs. Sometimes you've just made yourself too inaccessible to people like you. You may not be having friendly encounters with other single people on your street because nobody on your street has been single for twenty years, or not having them with people in your office because you're not doing the work you were meant to do. Probably the most dramatic change that ever occurred in my own romantic life followed my move from tweedy Cambridge to cosmopolitan Beacon Hill. Almost overnight, my prospects seemed to increase exponentially. I suspect that Cambridge just had a few too many students to provide very good prospects for the experienced professional I had become. Nice as it was to run into Archibald Cox on the way to the cleaner's, I was more in my element on Beacon Hill's gaslit streets, which attracted more people like me.

If you're convinced that you're in the right place, and as attractive as you can be, you may want to try to send more overtly sexual signals. Pick out someone at a cocktail party and look steadily into his or her eyes. Look away for a while, then look back again. Keep doing this until one of you starts to smile or begins a conversation. Try, above all, to keep thinking on your feet. One woman I know occasionally shared an elevator with a man she found attractive. One day he bumped into her in a rush to avoid a rapidly closing door. Flustered, he began to apologize until she reassured him with a smile. "Oh, please don't apologize," she insisted. "I rather enjoyed it." (On another such occasion, the woman tells me she said: "Oh, please don't apologize—I've been hoping you'd do that for weeks.") A casual encounter immediately took on a new cast that led to their getting together for coffee within a week.

Some experts suggest that single people search for love via such indirect routes as taking courses or visiting museums, where romance is supposed to lurk, along with the Rauschenbergs. This advice, though well meaning, strikes me as problematic. I guess it's partly because I've had such dismal luck trying to follow it. It seems that, if you do anything mostly to find dates, they almost never turn up, whereas if you do something for the fun of it they emerge serendipitously. The best place for single New Yorkers to meet kindred spirits, for instance, is supposed to be at the Museum of Modern Art on a Sunday afternoon. I went there for years, hoping to corral a few dates, and found a love affair only with *Guernica*—and even it ended badly when the painting was shipped to Madrid. And then there's another drawback to searching for romance by taking adult ed courses or by visiting museums. Doing so tends to co-opt great pleasures by turning them into often futile exercises in looking for love.

A better approach to revitalizing your love life involves going after what you want directly, without coming on so aggressively that you scare everybody away. Think of yourself as a management consultant brought in to review your possible romantic options. What might Booz, Allen suggest that you haven't already tried?

One answer is to look toward many of the new dating options that have gained credibility only recently, such as the personals ads, professional matchmaking services, and the new electronic mail exchanges (which often turn out to provide some male and female exchanges as well). All of these seem to me to have one immense advantage over just about everything else you can name: they attract people who are, by definition, looking for romance as avidly as you are. Put your friends on Red Alert for blind dates and they may come up with none until Pearl Harbor Day rolls around. Go to cocktail parties and you may glance lovingly at the Brie en croûte but not much else. Work on a political campaign and you may do your part for democracy while dating gets left out in the cold.

But when you take out a personals ad or join a video-dating service, you know that you will at least have access to a pool of others who are certifiably interested in love with a capital L. And that, to my mind, makes them far more honest and appealing than many other activities you can engage in, including snuggling up to Nautilus machines mostly in the hope that they will leave you snuggling up to somebody else instead. Besides, many of the new options can be a lot of fun—not to mention far less expensive than state-of-the-art health club memberships. And, if they don't leave you with the love affair of the decade, they can leave you with new friends and experiences (which is, to a large extent, what being single is all about). Wouldn't you really rather try one of them than yet another interminable blind date with somebody your cousin knew in veterinary school?

The Personals Touch

The best of the new options for most people is taking out a personals ad in a reputable magazine or newspaper. Most ads are so inexpensive—often costing as little as a dollar or two a line—that you have almost nothing to lose by running one. Nobody I know has failed to get his or her money's worth, and that goes for me, too. One ad that ran for several weeks in the Boston *Phoenix* brought me more inquiries from interesting men than I'd had all year. (The ad cost thirty dollars, which might sound like a lot, until you consider that it is probably less than what you'd spend on dinner for two in a restaurant, on one of those blind dates you always wish would end with the shrimp cocktail.) I heard from some fifty men in all: a doctor, a musician, an architect, a technical writer, a journalist, and from three lawyers and a half dozen academic types, to name some. I'd have loved to meet many of them but never got around to it, because the first person who answered my ad turned out to be a sweet, funny, lovable, handsome Harvard-educated lawyer who'd also been an Eagle Scout and student council president . . . a man who immediately caused me to lose interest in following up on the others. A lot of my friends asked me why a man so attractive "needed" to use the personals and the answer is that he didn't need to. He has a busy and happy life and presumably could have gotten dates in other ways, just as I presumably could have although, for some reason, I hadn't. *(My* only excuse was that I had been holed up in my apartment for a year writing this book, which turned out to be the equivalent of slow death by strangulation for my love life.) My new friend simply realized that there are far more efficient ways of finding prospective dates than by going to noisy cocktail parties, or risking a conflict of interest by asking out your clients, or trying to pick somebody up at Bloomingdale's. So he passed up the other ways of getting what he hoped for and, fortunately for me, turned to the personals.

If thousands of other men and women are finding that it pays to advertise, they are also discovering new places to go public. Not long ago, personals columns appeared mostly in such starchy publications as the *New York Review of Books* —not much help for somebody who lived in Skokie or thought the *Alexandria Quartet* was a new-wave rock band. The columns turn up today in a spectrum of magazines and newspapers so broad that it appeals to almost every special interest.

The best idea is to place an ad in a publication that attracts people like you, or one that you read and enjoy regularly. The ideal places for successful professionals to advertise, for instance, tend to be in well-established city magazines such as *New York, Philadelphia,* and the *Washingtonian.* Almost all such publications attract readers as well heeled as they are smart. One city magazine that recently launched a personals section found that its subscribers had a median income of $41,000, not entirely surprising since more than eighty percent attended college.

Other publications, however, aren't to be overlooked. Even the left-of-center *Village Voice* seems to draw a surprisingly traditional group of advertisers. Many are doctors, lawyers, dentists, or members of other respected professions. A survey of one thousand users of the personals columns in the *Voice* turned up some interesting statistics. Its typical male advertiser is thirty-one, makes $35,000 a year, and receives thirteen or fourteen responses to an ad. Its typical female advertiser is thirty, makes $29,000 a year, and gets some fifty responses to an ad. (Most publications say, incidentally, that women do get more replies than do men, who still seem more ready to take the initiative in seeking dates.) Other publications carry personals columns that attract readers with more specialized interests. Even the venerable *Harvard* magazine, for members and friends of the Harvard University community, now accepts personals ads from alumni and others.

Although many people fear that the personals ads will attract losers, the statistics suggest the opposite: that they increasingly attract *winners*. A lot of successful men and women are too busy to make dates any other way. Some people fear that the ads they respond to will prove untruthful, but even this worry seems exaggerated. The *Voice* executives who surveyed their personals users found that more than seventy percent said they met people who *did* match their descriptions of themselves.

A final reason or two for using the personals might be the obvious. Some of us who are single feel a little like hard-to-adopt children; in spite of our many lovable qualities, something makes romance harder to find for us than for other people. A five-foot-ten woman or a five-foot-two man often has trouble finding dates with whom he or she can see eye to eye, on more levels than one. The personals ads let you put your less-than-common denominators up front and can thereby go a long way toward turning up somebody who can live with them. A female friend of mine in her mid-forties listened enviously to my experiences with the personals but remained convinced that her age made them impractical for her; she finally wrote an ad nonetheless—and she, too, was completely smitten by the first man who answered her ad.

Not the least of the advantages of the personals is that, even if you're not looking for romance, you can still use such columns to advertise for a fourth for bridge or a crew member for your sailboat, a practice becoming increasingly common in publications around the country. Some new services will even help you compose your personals ad if you've always been a little shy about singing your own praises on paper. Look for ads for the services on the pages of the magazines and newspapers with personals columns in the back.

In any case, observe a few safety guidelines whenever you advertise. Never put your home phone number in an ad but have all replies sent to a box number provided by the publication your ad appears in. When responding to someone else's ad, write a short upbeat note that includes only your first name and home phone number, never an address or a last name that appears in the phone book. That way, you're protected from the rare kook or crazy who might decide to turn up at your door. After all, you can always get your phone number changed easily, but it's much harder to move to a new apartment or office. And does anybody really need to be told never to invite a stranger to your home for the first date, no matter how promising a phone call sounded? Meeting at a coffee shop usually proves easier, not just on your wallet, but on your nervous system.

Not-So-Blind Dates

Not everybody, of course, relishes the idea of boosting his or her love life by running ads on the same pages that often carry listings for used VW diesels or belly dancers who make house calls, which is why other dating aids are on the increase. Your next best bet after the personals columns might be a visit to a professional matchmaking service. (Look for these and other sorts of dating aids mentioned here under "Dating Services" in your Yellow Pages or on the pages of any glossy city magazine.) As anybody who's seen *Fiddler on the Roof* knows, professional matchmakers have long had an honored place in countries outside the United States. Arranged marriages, or at least arranged meetings, have always been common in the Far East, India, and Israel—not to mention in Orthodox Jewish communities in New York and elsewhere.

Now professional matchmakers are making their presence felt across the United States, with a new twist. They aim less to attract people of a particular nationality or religion than to serve sophisticated professionals who have little time to meet people in other ways. It's probably no coincidence that a lot of their clients are professionals who are used to employing management consultants on the job and who are now doing the same sort of thing outside the office.

The professional matchmakers generally request that you submit a photo and biography or résumé, then be interviewed by a staff member who'll want to know more about you. A fee, ranging from about thirty dollars to more than three hundred dollars, gets you an agreed-upon number of dates with people handpicked for you. Among the better-known matchmaking services are Mary the Matchmaker, on the West Coast, and the Godmothers, in the East; other services, such as Lunch Dates and Lunch Partners, specialize in getting people together for casual meals or drinks in restaurants.

Of course, there can be glitches, with these services as with any others. One dating bureau finds itself swamped with the résumés of terrific women—and practically begging for those of attractive men. So it's not a bad idea to ask about the size of the pool from which matches will be drawn and never to shell out a hefty sum unless you're guaranteed access to more people than you'd meet at a neighbor's cocktail party. Still, professional matchmakers have something important going for them: the chance to tap personal intuition. Nothing substitutes for it in matters of the heart, and when your friends' hunches about blind dates don't seem to pan out, a pro's just might.

Another good bet can be using one of the new video-dating services, such as Great Expectations, on the West Coast, and the People Network, in the East. Most services operate on a set of simple principles. All you do is visit one of their offices, where a staff member makes a short tape of you talking about yourself and what you want in someone else. If you're shy about opening up, a staff member can interview you on tape to get you going. Your videotape then goes into a central file, to which subscribers of the other sex have access. You can look at their files, too. When you come across a tape of somebody you'd like to meet, you give that person's code number to a staff member. The better services tend to use numbers instead of names to protect subscribers' privacy. The person you'd like to meet is then notified of your interest and comes in to view your tape. If the attraction proves to be mutual, the two of you receive each other's names and phone numbers, and either party can make the first call. Therein, however, lies the hitch, which is that the attraction may never be mutual or be so far less often than you'd like. Video dating inevitably tends to favor the gorgeous and quick-witted. Cocktail parties favor the same people, and, if you'd had any luck at *them*, you might not need to try a dating service. One attractive and charming woman told me that it felt brutal to request to meet five men, only to find that none was interested in her. Then there is the not inconsiderable expense of video dating, usually at least several hundred dollars, which can make the loss seem even greater.

Even the cost of video dating, however, may bring a few advantages with it. A lot of people want to go out with someone at least solvent, if not outright affluent. The high cost of video dating might also attract clients who are more serious about romance than someone who's paid only a dollar or two a line to run a personals ad in a newspaper. One satisfied user said: "I felt that the high price tag did draw people who were looking for a long-term relationship. Who would be crazy enough to pay close to a thousand dollars just for a one-night stand?"

And then there is something else, which is that most of us really do want to like the looks of our dates. I've met countless single men and women who insist that appearances couldn't interest them in the least—that what they really care about in a date are things like warmth, intelligence, and a working sense of humor. Yet, once they get those things, they still feel dissatisfied, claiming the "chemistry" isn't right. To the extent that looks have always formed part of that oh-so-elusive intangible, video dating might help you find it more quickly than anything else.

Finally, if making a tape doesn't produce your perfect paramour, it can help you see yourself as some of your prospects might. One woman admitted that video dating didn't help her in the least to find true love, but it did motivate her to lose twenty pounds, which helped her to find romance on a beach in Martinique. And the same sorts of safety guidelines that apply to the personals ads ought to be observed here, too. Author Tracy Cabot, who tried video dating and wrote about it for a magazine, didn't have much trouble passing up an encounter with a man who said that he enjoyed "taping the spirit voices of the dead." Trust your own vibes about who might—and might not—work out.

A home computer fan might also check out the new electronic mail exchanges that can serve as technological cupids. An electronic mail exchange, to which you gain access by subscribing to an information service, essentially allows you to run a personals ad regionally or even nationwide by feeding a message directly from your home computer into a broad network of others. Subscriptions can be expensive, because they may also include such things as news reports or the latest Dow Jones averages. And not all information services are set up to be conduits for such messages. One company that does offer that and other services is Source Telecomputing Corporation, 1616 Anderson Road, McLean, Virginia 22102.

How do the new electronic networks work? Let's say you'd like to meet single people in the Northeast who sometimes get to Manhattan on weekends and enjoy Broadway shows. You write up a little description of what you are looking for, then send it out to the others who subscribe to the information service you do; you do this by using a communications software program, such as PC Talk, and a modem, which hooks your home computer up to your telephone. Interested men or women respond directly to you, and you talk to each other by tapping messages into your computer. Subscribers have identifying numbers you can use until you feel comfortable enough to give out your name. Although not for everybody, these mail exchanges might one day replace personals ads as the most efficient way to reach many prospective dates.

None of this should be taken as suggesting that many of the more old-fashioned methods of connecting can't work, too. The computer dating services that attracted so much attention in the early 1970s, for instance, are still around and are usually listed in the phone book under "Dating Services." For a small fee, a computer dating service will usually send you a standardized form on which you provide basic information about yourself and your preferences for dates. Filling out the form is a little like taking a multiple-choice test. Then your answers are electronically scanned for the names of possible matches, and the service sends you a set number of these. One drawback to computer dating is that it is inevitably less precise than things like personals ads, which let you describe your wants in more detail than canned forms do. But it, too, is worth considering because who knows where love will turn up?

And what about the singles bars that are everybody's least favorite way of meeting? I have to admit that I have a good word even for them, though it wasn't always so.

Even as a college student who had yet to sign her first lease, I fervently believed one thing: nobody was going to catch me in one of those tacky singles bars, where the most interesting thing you were likely to come home with was a swizzle stick shaped like a tennis racquet or perhaps a plastic coconut with a parasol sticking out of it. Naturally, I planned to have dates, but I was going to meet them in ways more compatible with my personality. If I couldn't meet men by attending social events—lectures, museum openings, and such—I would resort to more traditional techniques, such as twisting the arms of friends for the names of relatives, or making witty remarks in front of the zucchini bin at Stop & Shop, where with any luck an intriguing man would overhear. Not surprisingly, there were problems with my approach to dating; quite simply, it often left me without dates.

Noticing that singles bars were packing people in not far from my apartment, I never actually got up the nerve to walk into one of them cold. But I did get an assignment to keep a diary of my experiences in them. Like Nelly Bly infiltrating mental hospitals, I would check out the bars under a presumably safe cover.

As things turned out, I never did go out with any of the unattached men I met in places like Kitty Hawks. But I did meet men I *could* have dated and that, in itself, was a surprise. I also found singles bars easier on my nervous system than expected. Some people say that what you experience there can be the equivalent of a sort of visual rape. But since I never felt that my ego or body was on the line—only that my journalistic skills were—I never felt like a human prime rib who'd stood up and walked into a meat market. If you are shy about trying a singles bar—or, for that matter, any of the other new dating methods mentioned here—pretend you're writing an article about your own experiences for a local newspaper. Or just go with a friend who can give you moral support.

It also seems that, if you visit singles bars, your attitude makes a lot of difference. Go looking for little more than a chance to unwind after work and you probably won't come away feeling like Triple A beef on the hoof. Go looking for Mr. or Ms. Till Death Do Us Part, and you may feel not just dehumanized but repeatedly defeated as well.

As for me, I was glad to have an excuse to try singles bars, though I never went back. I probably wouldn't try a singles bar at fifty-two, so I'm glad I did at twenty-two. I also liked the idea that I may one day be able to tell my children or grandchildren, or at least a few nieces and nephews, that I experienced first hand an American cultural phenomenon. I've actually been to Maxwell's Plum and not just seen it in the movies. I even found myself feeling a bit smug when talking to single friends who never ventured into such places, sounding perhaps a bit like a draftee who brags about bravery in the foxholes. Then again, I am the sort of person who, if married, would no doubt drag my spouse to heart-shaped bathtubs in the Poconos or to weekend "marriage encounters" where they give you bumper stickers with hearts entwined like wedding rings, just to be *sure* I hadn't missed anything. Your tastes in fun may run more to doing one of the other things I mentioned, or just to going alone to a premiere of *La Forza del Destino,* where, with any luck, *destino* will plunk you down next to the man or woman of your dreams.

What all of this seems to add up to is that there exist more ways than ever before of looking for romance, and one is probably right for you. You may not be the sort to go chasing after destiny, but you can still find an activity that lets you meet destiny halfway.

If none of the new dating services holds a strong appeal, consider that you may even be better off without a raging love affair on your hands. Nowhere is it written that you can't spend a perfectly charming Saturday evening taking your niece to the *Icecapades* or having dinner with a college roommate.

What matters is that, when you do connect with someone special, you decide the wait was worth it. Look for somebody who sees the best in you and loses no opportunity to bring it out. And don't settle for a dreary "relationship" when what you really want is romance, because if you settle for too long you may forget that anything else even exists.

Dating, ultimately, ought to be *fun*, or why bother with it at all? Some people work so hard at their romances that you feel they ought to become eligible for unemployment benefits when they're over. A love affair should always leave you feeling better about yourself and enjoying life more than you did before. A romance that doesn't leave you feeling that way might give you the best reason you'll ever have for trying one of the new techniques I've mentioned and finding somebody who appreciates you for the uniquely fascinating person that you are.

You'll need a bit of luck, of course, to meet someone you'll enjoy seeing often. But, as Stanley Marcus, chairman emeritus of Neiman-Marcus, has said: *"Luck* comes to those searching for something." And even if you don't find what you are looking for, you will almost certainly come home with some good stories to tell your nieces and nephews. First, there was the hot air balloonist who wanted you to get high together . . .

5

Keeping Company

No small portion of the life of every unattached adult ought to be devoted to going to parties, for reasons that should be obvious. Parties bring out the best in everyone but a misanthropist. They allow you to wear your best clothes and practice your best lines beforehand in the bathroom mirror. They also allow you to make an appearance only a short time after having had divers parts of your body enhanced for the occasion by hairdressers, manicurists, and other professionals who charge only slightly less than the national debt of Brazil for their services.

But parties do more than allow you to present your best face to the world. To be happily single, you need to form strong ties to lots of kindred spirits, and you don't meet them holed up in your apartment. Parties let you connect with a broader cross section of people than you otherwise would be able to.

You'll notice, however, that I've said *people* and not *men* or *women*. Unattached adults who dislike parties generally do so for one reason: they see them as opportunities primarily to meet prospective dates, who turn up less frequently than is usually desired. The result is that they often believe they have wasted an entire evening, because it hasn't brought them any closer to the lasting love that they believe they want. The problem is, in their unceasing efforts to find dates, often by talking only to attractive members of the other sex, they overlook all sorts of other interesting guests who might nonetheless have made the evening worthwhile. At parties, as in life itself, the best way to have fun is to stop beating the bushes for what isn't there and just enjoy what *is*.

That having been said, you can't enjoy any party if you don't get invited to it. So it's probably worth noting that there are at least four good ways of insuring that you will get to attend a lot of them:

1. Have a lot of solvent and outgoing friends.
2. Give many parties yourself so that people will feel obligated to pay you back.
3. Join many clubs and organizations.
4. Watch the newspapers for announcements about glitzy parties that, though given by people or organizations you aren't familiar with, can nonetheless be attended by anyone.

The first option, that of having a lot of solvent and outgoing friends, is by far the best, simply because it will get you far more than party invitations. The trouble is that, especially when you are young, such acquaintances can be hard to come by. A chilly reality of singlehood is that people who expect their friends to invite them to parties are often disappointed, especially if many of their friends are married and treat every social event they host as an opportunity to stock the Ark. By all means, go to your friends' galas, but never expect to go to as many as you'd like.

The second option, that of giving a lot of parties of your own, is naturally one that you should pursue. But all sorts of things can work against your hosting enough of them to make a real difference in your social life: lack of time, lack of money, and lack of an apartment bigger than a Wheaties box, to name a few. And good manners have fallen by the wayside to such a degree that fewer people every year feel any compunction to pay back most of the invitations they have received. Then again, *giving* parties is an art form unto itself, which is why it will be discussed a little later.

The third route to getting invited to parties, joining groups, bears a bit more explanation than it might appear to need. You may belong to a lot of organizations already but still not be going to nearly so many social events as might be desired. In that case, you may have joined the wrong kind (at least for the purposes under consideration here). Membership in a local camera club, for instance, is a great way to learn why you came back from Antigua with so many double exposures. But what it will get you in the way of invitations probably isn't much; maybe one for an annual Christmas party and one for a summer outing. More significantly, the people you'll meet at those parties are likely to be people you'd meet anyway at regular club meetings.

To get a lot of party invitations from groups, you've got to join some really large ones. Membership has to be big enough so that any social event is virtually certain to turn up some people you haven't met before. Especially worth joining are neighborhood associations, political campaign committees, professional and trade organizations, college alumni/ae groups, and broadly based social clubs. Also worth checking out are the more narrowly focused organizations discussed in the sections of this book most closely related to their underlying purposes (for example, the Appalachian Mountain Club and American Youth Hostels, Inc., covered in the chapter on travel).

Joining a nationally known group devoted to a worthy cause, or your local chapter of the same, has an added benefit: the outfit often will sell its membership list to groups that serve a similar interest, so you will get invited to all of their parties, too. Membership in many such organizations can frequently be had for a modest twenty-five dollars a year or less, scarcely enough to keep you in sour-cream-curry dip for parties of your own. Almost any such groups that you join can do far more than get you invited to social events, but they are among the fringe benefits even so.

Finally, your last option, that of watching newspapers for notices of upcoming parties open to the public, is one far too many single people overlook. They ignore them partly because such social events tend to be written up on what used to be called the "society pages" of a local publication, or in sections that many readers skip over en route to the sports columns or TV listings. The New York *Times*, for one, posts notices of upcoming parties in the "Future Events" section of the Sunday paper, surrounded by the engagement announcements of postdebs. All of this means that you may really have to look hard for details of get-togethers that might interest you.

Then, too, a lot of the parties you'll read about will be too expensive to consider unless you are the sort of person who gets written up in all of those articles in *Town and Country* magazine that probably ought to be titled, "How to Be Happily Single on $100,000 a Year." The thing to remember here is that most newspapers list not just the two-hundred-and-fifty-dollar-a-plate roast beef dinners but far less expensive charity benefits, where you may be able to get all the white-wine spritzers you can drink for a mere ten or twenty dollars. In spite of their lower cost, the latter can be even more fun than the higher-priced events, because they tend to attract a younger crowd of people whose social consciences click with yours.

Apart from these time-tested ways of getting invited to parties, a few others are worth noting briefly. If the arts interest you, one excellent way to get invited to a lot of parties is to go around to every art gallery in your town and sign its guest book or ask a staff member to add your name to its mailing list. (The latter will generally be done more readily after you have asked a few bright questions about the works hanging on the walls, suggesting that you may one day be interested in taking one home.) Once you have somehow gotten on the mailing list for a gallery, you will likely get invited to upward of a half dozen or more exhibit openings a year, where you are likely to meet any number of charming young artists smelling faintly of gesso—not to mention a lot of their friends.

Modern art and photography showcases tend to attract a younger set than do those specializing in the likes of ancestral portraits or little-known Winslow Homers. The more offbeat the gallery, the more likely its staff members also tend to be to add a few extra names to its mailing list, so don't hesitate to poke around in places where you see works that will never make it into the Louvre. Joining *museums* can also get you a lot of invitations to openings, and many of these have "junior councils" or "young people's committees" that offer people in their twenties or thirties a good way to get more involved in their affairs. In my part of the country few events attract more certified Yuppies than do openings at Boston's Institute of Contemporary Art, housed in a converted fire station.

Not to neglect the obvious: it's also important to get invited *back* to the homes of friends who have been kind enough to invite you to their soirees, so make a special effort to express your appreciation for having been included. Begin by always trying to respond to any invitation to a private party within forty-eight hours of receiving it. Even if you aren't sure you'll be able to attend, at least call to say that and that you'll be in touch again the moment your plans are definite. An iffy reply lets your hosts know that their invitations have arrived and may spare them weeks of wondering whether yours has gone astray or you are just too disorganized to acknowledge its arrival. It may help to remember that food and liquor often have to be ordered weeks before a party, especially a catered one. Prompt RSVPs, even if tentative, allow a party-giver to make adjustments in quantity while it's still possible.

If you are unable to attend a private party you'd like to have gone to, call to express your regrets, then write a short note to emphasize how happy you were to receive the invitation. A handwritten message still conveys the most warmth. If you have one done by a secretary, anyway, have it done on your personal or plain stationery, with no typist's initials at the bottom.

When you do attend a party, praise it lavishly. It ought always to be possible to approach a host or hostess at some point during the evening and say, "This is a *fabulous* party," or to say something enthusiastic about the food, the strawberry daiquiris, or the guests. Then thank the party-giver again when you are leaving—a courtesy that a scandalous number of single people either neglect or perform in such a perfunctory manner that it scarcely counts. It's thoughtful to go around to the other people you have enjoyed meeting, too, and to say good-bye to them as well, which also gives you a last opportunity to exchange business cards if you haven't done so.

Within twenty-four hours after a party has ended, either call the host to say again how much you appreciated his or her efforts or write a lovely thank you note in which you try to be specific about what you liked most. (Yes, I've set down a lot of "rules" here, but the assumption behind them is that you'll follow them, if you do so at all, not because you *have* to but because you *want* to get invited back—and these are the things that will help to insure that you do.) The custom of sending flowers to the host the morning after you have attended his or her party has fallen sorely into disuse, partly because of its expense. Yet, for that reason among others, it can make a tremendously favorable impression. It can also restore you quite quickly to the good graces of someone whose party you have been forced to bow out of at the last minute.

In expressing your gratitude for a party invitation, try especially to avoid that embarrassing expression: "I really enjoyed myself." You didn't enjoy *yourself*, you enjoyed the *party.* Saying that you "enjoyed" yourself also tends to leave the impression that you spent the entire evening committing God knows what autoerotic acts in the bathroom, while everybody else was quite innocently carving up the Camembert.

Innocent Parties—and
Some Not-So-Innocent Ones

The inevitable result of going to a lot of parties is that you will feel impelled to give a few of your own. You need not, of course, return every invitation you receive. But sooner or later you will have to express your gratitude for all the galas you have attended by a means other than fulsome expressions of thanks or even bouquets of posies delivered the morning after an event. You will need, in short, to give a few parties of your own.

By "parties" I simply mean events that involve you and one or two other people to whom you are not related or otherwise irrevocably obligated. I suppose that, when you are toting up the list of parties you have hosted in the past year, you could count the time you put up your fifth cousins from Sioux Falls for the night after their flight was canceled . . . or the time you gave your landlord a beer in return for help getting your drainpipes unclogged . . . or the time you fixed a seductive little dinner for somebody who turned out to have a spouse and kids back home. But that wouldn't seem quite right, would it? The kind of events you really want to credit to your account are a little more—well, *fun.*

Admittedly, giving parties can be expensive, not to mention harrowing and exhausting. I couldn't begin to count the near disasters that flared up during my own early attempts at gracious entertaining. I recall one party to which I invited three people who turned out to be suing the guest of honor . . . another at which I painstakingly laid out dozens of museum-quality cocktail napkins but forgot to put towels in the bathroom . . . and yet another when my downstairs neighbor called the cops the first time I invited home everybody from the office.

Those experiences alone were enough to make me consider taking early retirement from the local party circuit. Yet I continued to entertain often, and I'm glad I did. Giving a lot of parties has helped me to make a lot of friends of both sexes. It's also helped to polish my social skills and get my apartment cleaned before someone called the health inspector. And it can do other things, including providing one of the most reliable means you have of forging an honorary family. A family consists of people who know and love you as well as they know and love each other. Often as not, they won't be able to do either unless you bring them together frequently. A family also consists of people who share rituals, traditions, and memories. Those can be born at your social events perhaps more easily than anywhere else.

Not to neglect the obvious, parties can also be a lot of fun, partly because you are free to give them in your own delightfully whimsical way. You are free to round up a dozen friends on impulse to play Trivial Pursuit or to pop popcorn as you catch a rerun of *Annie Hall* on TV. Nobody who is single needs first to clear such projects with a spouse, who may have longed to spend the evening quietly going over a batch of feasibility studies.

Developing a specialty can make entertaining that much easier. One woman thrives on fireside buffets for six to eight people, another does best by having a dozen or two over for a cookout. A divorced man I know has carved out a secure social niche by giving what he calls an annual "eligibles bash" every February around Valentine's Day. The only rule is that absolutely no entrenched couples are allowed on the scene but only people who are looking for someone new. (The host claims the party has resulted in two marriages so far with another in the wings.) Another man annually throws open the doors of the architectural firm in which he is a partner for a few hours after work. The Luxo lamps shed their light on wheels of cheese, alongside baskets of figs and grapes, that he orders in for the event.

Giving parties, if only for one or two other people, can be as vital to your emotional health as getting exercise is to your physical health. So you need to do it almost as often as you swim or play tennis. I try to set little quotas for myself to insure that I'll never go too long without opening my doors to somebody else, a practice you might adopt. I would try to have somebody over for drinks or dinner at least once a week. Give a dinner party every month or so—more if you can afford it—and have a larger party once or twice a year, perhaps on your own birthday, to sweep in all the people you haven't managed to corral any other way. Another tradition might be the sort of party you enjoy giving most, such as a clambake with seaweed packed into a metal garbage can instead of into a sand pit.

Whom should you invite? One of the great luxuries of singlehood is that you can eliminate from your social life the people you aren't wild about. (This, of course, excludes relatives and possibly a few others, such as the best friends of a man or woman with whom you are involved.) So the cardinal rule of entertaining when you are single is to invite people over because you *want* to and never because you feel you should. You will have enough time after you are married to play host to people who make you crazy, from your in-laws to your spouse's clients. If there are people whom you dislike but must entertain for one reason or another, why not have one party a year just for all of *them*— and let all of them talk to each other? Don't inflict them on the people who have been wonderful to you and who have, therefore, done nothing to deserve such punishment.

I'm especially inclined to banish from my guest lists people who are rude, not merely to me but to anybody. Nothing causes a party-giver more worry than wondering whether the people you have tried so hard to put at ease will wind up getting bruised by one of your other guests. The people you want to fill your life with aren't rude to anybody, ever, let alone before your eyes, and in front of your own fire.

I'm also inclined to pass up the chance to entertain people who are simply tedious. Lots of party-givers invite them on the grounds that they are basically harmless. I believe that chronic bores are not harmless in the least! Their tediousness almost always results from their lack of interest in other people, and, if they aren't interested in you, why should you be interested in *them*? Another problem with inviting deadbeats is that they sap your energy as a host or hostess, because they require you always to be on the look-out for the guests who need to be rescued from them. A long-divorced woman who has become one of New York's most celebrated hostesses admitted in a recent interview that her parties have gained renown partly because she makes a huge effort to eliminate soporific people. That, she added, means inviting few couples, because there exist very few couples in which both people are really interesting. I seem to be lucky, knowing a lot of twosomes in which both people hold their own quite nicely. If I didn't, however, I'd line up squarely behind the New York hostess and see the fifty percenters privately but not at my parties.

Apart from ridding your parties of people who will drag others down along with them, my "invite only people you like" rule has something else going for it, which serves as a handy barometer of your social life in general. If you don't know enough people whom you'd like to have over for a large party, the solution isn't to squander your time and energy on those whom you don't: it's to go out and find some new friends whom you will always love to see.

And now a few words about specific kinds of parties you can give (not counting birthday and holiday ones, which need to be seen in their own context and which I'll therefore get to a little later):

The Dinner Party

A dinner party is always a consummately grown-up affair, only one reason why it is my own favorite form of entertaining. At a dinner party, however small, candles and flowers are allowed. Elegant clothes can be worn, and subjects not fit for children's ears can be introduced. Perhaps no other diversion permits you to sample simultaneously so many of life's greatest pleasures: good food, good wine, good music, and, above all, good conversation. A fine dinner party is nothing if not civilized. And that's something you can scarcely say about a noisy cocktail party for a hundred people, all drinking wine from plastic cups and listening to acid rock.

I am especially fond of smaller dinners—for, say, seven or eight guests. This sort of event has just about everything going for it. It isn't too expensive, too time-consuming, or too hard to pull off. Nobody gets left out of the conversation or denied a chance to meet anybody else, because you can easily keep an eye on all of the guests at once and skillfully draw out the person who needs a little bit of coaxing. Invite fewer than six guests and the conversation may lag if one or two don't click; invite more than eight and your dinner party is likely to break down into several splinter groups. A smallish party also doesn't require you to spend too much time cleaning up afterward, such as by vacuuming the Dorito crumbs out of a sofa at 4 A.M. so the cockroaches won't have gotten to them by seven.

Dinner parties of any size have something else going for them, too, and it is that they teach you how to cook. Your guests force you to learn how to prepare something resembling real food, and, with any luck, you'll soon be tempted to make some of it just for yourself.

It goes without saying that a dinner party can be a wonderful way to make somebody feel loved and pampered, especially when it turns out to be an event just for two. It is also a blessing that women no longer have a monopoly in this department. Single men have probably cooked for me more meals than I've cooked for them, and I can unequivocally assert that none has ever hurt his chances with me by turning out to cook like Paul Prudhomme's long-lost twin brother. Nor have I heard of any other woman who dropped a man because he fed her sole Veronique with new potatoes, steamed asparagus and a salad, and cherries jubilee.

Guest lists for small dinner parties ought to be drawn up more carefully than any others. The etiquette books brim with hints about inviting people with similar interests— about, for instance, the advisability of combining a man who has just climbed Mount McKinley with a woman who's climbed Annapurna. Such advice no doubt has its merits. Yet I have also found that it can backfire. The stockbrokers you invited in hopes they would have some shared interests may turn out to have almost too much to say to each other, going on about IPOs and P/E ratios until everybody's eyes glaze over like the crème caramel. I have found that people's relation to one another is more important than their relation to a subject. You don't want anybody to get stranded, having no one to talk to but you. Neither do you want most people to be able to talk only to those they see all the time already. (That's why the dinner parties married couples give in suburbia can turn out to be so dreary.) So I try, when inviting guests, to make sure that each one will know at least one other person—but also that each one will *not* know at least one other person. Always injecting a new personality or two keeps your parties from getting stale and your friends looking forward to returning to them.

What you'll serve at a dinner party will depend, of course, on your income and your tastes. Try, in any case, to perfect at least one main dish that can be prepared well before the event and popped into the oven at the last minute. Single people who live alone often can give weeknight dinner parties only if they do most of the cooking the night before.

Otherwise, there is always the risk that you will get tied up on the subway and have no time to prepare for them. So look especially for dishes that you can make the day before and will prove even better on the second. Many wonderful lamb and veal stews fall into this category. So do chili and tomato-based spaghetti sauces. One currently fashionable dish that can be made in advance is the rich French casserole called cassoulet, made with white beans and sausage or pork, and often lamb or duck.

Never hesitate, in any case, to supplement your own efforts with sauces or other items from gourmet takeout shops. It is practically impossible when you are single to serve an elegant dinner at which you have made every course from scratch, and I believe it is madness even to try. I'm not sure I've ever given a dinner party at which I made every item myself. Sometimes I just pick up a few appetizers, such as marinated vegetables, and a dessert from a bakery. Often, however, I lean on takeout foods more heavily. I recently served the following meal to a group of seven dinner guests: fresh pasta with puttanesca sauce, garlic bread, salad, wine, and amaretto ice cream with cookies to eat with freshly brewed hot coffee. The pasta and sauce for my meal came from a Charles Street carry-out food store called Pasta Pronto. The amaretto ice cream came home with me from a sweet shop named Il Dolce Momento. The cookies began life in an excellent commercial bakery. I prepared only the garlic bread and the salad of ruby lettuce and sliced fresh mushrooms, dressed with a zingy vinaigrette. The entire meal took a total of about thirty minutes to pull together, not counting the time for shopping.

I also frequently bring home an unbaked deep-dish pizza or two, which can be kept in the freezer or refrigerator until the guests arrive. You can buy excellent unbaked pizzas at the restaurants called Pizzeria Uno, which started in Chicago and have spread to the East. I have found that friends almost never feel shortchanged when they find themselves on the receiving end of this sort of informal meal. In fact, many seem to feel liberated by it, knowing that, since I've served pizza to them, they are free to do the same to me.

Try, in any case, not to worry too much about serving the same thing too many times. I am always reading articles in *Vogue* or *Town and Country* about hostesses who keep little books listing what they've served to their guests, primarily so that they can avoid ever making the same thing again. This practice seems less a way of feeding guests' stomachs than of feeding hostesses' egos. If you served something for which your guests went back for thirds, why not do them a favor and serve it again? And do yourself a favor by not having to strain to perfect a new dish each time. If serving veal normande to the same guests three times in a row will enable you to feel relaxed and attentive to their needs, I say more power to veal normande. I have been to my friend Kerry's house approximately eight times for dinner, and on at least six I have been served chicken tarragon with rice pilaf, steamed string beans, warm crescent rolls, and sherbet with lacy cookies for dessert. (To the best of my knowledge, Kerry had only one other dish besides chicken tarragon, a fish something-or-other that she makes for people who don't eat meat.) Does anybody love Kerry less because she serves the same thing repeatedly? Certainly not. And I, for one, admire her spunk for sticking to what she does best, instead of floating a gastronomic trial balloon every time someone turns up at the door.

The Dessert Party

"Party" might be too formal a word for this sort of delicious get-together. To give one you just invite people to drop by after dinner for coffee and dessert, homemade or from a bakery. Suggest that guests arrive around eight-thirty or nine if you live in a large city, earlier in small towns where the evening meal comes at five-thirty or six. A dessert party makes an especially nice way to entertain your older or more affluent friends, including all the two-income couples whose entertaining you could never hope to match on a course-by-course basis. Nobody can feel embarrassed about serving anybody a beautiful Linzer torte, a bourbon-pecan pie, a Black Forest chocolate cake, or even plates of blondies and brownies that have been named the best in your town by the local media. Offer the best vanilla ice cream you can afford with any of the preceding, and you will have given your friends a real treat that nonetheless cost far less than a several-course meal.

If you're so inclined, you might also put out fruit or cheese and crackers, or an after-dinner drink. I served Chéri Suisse for years—a liqueur I offered partly because guests like to splash it over the vanilla ice cream. I've since switched to Bailey's Irish Cream because it plays well in Boston, and also because I always serve it at my St. Patrick's Day feast and generally have some left over. A tiny glass of Bailey's also tends to satisfy a sweet tooth nicely and can keep you from devouring all of the other goodies you've put out for people who can afford the calories better than you can. The English serve postprandial glasses of port along with Stilton cheese and cream crackers or a heaping bowl of walnuts. This makes an especially nice way to entertain friends just back from trips to London or who aren't big on rich desserts.

It can also be fun to ask your guests to bring the after-dinner treats. One of the most successful parties I ever gave was a black-tie champagne and dessert gala to which every guest contributed his or her specialty. I labeled each offering with a place card so that others could ask for recipes ("Mary's Black-Bottom Pie," "Carolyn's Ambrosia," "Karen's Orange Cake," etc.). The only drinks besides champagne were coffee and Perrier for abstainers. Most people loved having a chance to dress up, and, because the desserts made the event special, I didn't feel I had to rent a ballroom to justify the fancy clothes.

The Cocktail Party

Unlike dinner parties, which have just about everything going for them, cocktail parties seem to me to have just about everything going against them. Their drawbacks include at least these: (1) they are expensive; (2) they require extensive planning; (3) they are often tedious and attended only out of duty; (4) they can wreak havoc with your furniture, not to mention your relations with the downstairs tenant; and (5) they virtually insure that you will have no chance to talk to your friends, which is practically the whole purpose of having a party. Add to these the reality that your apartment probably isn't big enough, you don't have enough chairs or wineglasses, and you get the vapors just from thinking about bringing six dozen people together at once—and I can't quite imagine why anyone would ever consider one seriously.

To be fair, I do think that giving a cocktail party can serve one slightly Machiavellian purpose not always to be overlooked. At various points during your single career you may meet someone whom you believe you would like to know better. Somehow, though, inviting that person over for crêpes St. Jacques by candlelight seems a bit much, as does giving a dinner party including several others. You'd like to connect again but in such a low-key way that the object of your attentions couldn't possibly read anything into your motives. The only answer, I'm afraid, is to give a largish party to which you invite that person along with many others. I did that once, and the man immediately piped up: "Oh, terrific, I'd love to come, and I'd also love to bring my fiancée." The approach I have just described, in other words, has its risks along with its merits, and you are well advised to consider both. But, when it works, it does so brilliantly, as evidenced by the growing number of couples I know who have one day gotten married after someone used a variant of this approach.

Here, then, are some tips on how to pull off a cocktail party, whatever your motives for giving one:

• Observe *especially* strictly the rule about inviting only people you like. The only thing worse than spending an evening with somebody who makes you crazy is spending an evening with fifty-seven people who make you crazy—and also slander your friends, spill Beaujolais on your white fur rug, and eat up all your $13.99-per-pound duck-and-pistachio pâté.

• Manage to get all your cleaning done before the day of the party. Check into the possibility of hiring a local cleaning service to do it for you, if you're busy. If you are going to subject yourself to the sort of nerve jangler a large cocktail party is, you need to save your strength for it.

• Don't feel you have to serve "cocktails" at a cocktail party. I rarely serve anything stronger than red and white wines, or champagne for fancy events, always along with soft drinks and bottled water and lime. I generally serve Robert Mondavi's Red and White Table Wines (nonvintage) because (1) they taste good; (2) they cost under $5.00; and (3) they come in a classy bottle. (The Mondavi Red and White are my house wines for dinner parties, too.) If you can afford more expensive French wines but aren't sure what to buy, stick to those produced by respected bottlers such as Louis Latour or Louis Jadot. I use bowl-shaped glass goblets for parties of two dozen people or less, move on to plastic when the event is very large.

• Make sure you can't afford to hire a caterer before you rule one out for the hors d'oeuvres. You may discover that the bland cheeses and crackers you pick up on your own can nonetheless seem to cost more than a state dinner for Margaret Thatcher. For the same amount, a caterer might come up with something far more interesting and throw in someone to help serve to boot. Even if you make your own food, a large cocktail party might require that you get someone to help serve. Deputize a friend for this purpose or consider hiring a student from a nearby college. Call its work-study office to ask how you can find one.

• Have something on the stereo for at least the first hour. After that, the place will get so noisy that nobody will even hear it. But, without a little music to soften things in the beginning, the early arrivals are likely to hear their voices bouncing off the walls. I am partial to piano music, which always seems perfect for a background: Scarlatti and Mozart for elegant dinner parties, Errol Garner and Keith Jarrett for looser ones that tend to draw a young crowd.

• Never worry that you've invited too many people to a cocktail party. The worst that could happen if you do is that some people will leave early, which is what some people will do anyway.

• On the other hand, expect at least twenty-five percent of all invited guests to decline. (At least, that's what one etiquette book I read said; it seems to me that the percentage at some of my own parties has been *higher.)* Expect even more not to attend if it snows or rains or if you ask people to dress up in the gorilla suits from their parents' attics. Also expect some people *not* to show up even if they have RSVP'd. Yes, it is an absolutely appalling display of bad manners. So please remember it the next time you, too, are tempted to bug out of a party at the last minute.

• Buy lots of ice. Even if you're only serving wine, you are unlikely to be able to keep all the whites chilled for the length of the party. And, if you're using your own cubes, be sure to empty out all your trays a few days before the party and fill them with fresh water. Like food, water can get stale, and your ice cubes can give a brackish taste to even the most expensive wines.

• Have on hand lots of beautiful cocktail napkins, which are very adult, and arrange them artfully in little fans and such to encourage people to use them. These can double nicely as coasters if you don't have enough for a huge crowd.

• Do not delude yourself into thinking that by not putting out ashtrays you will be making an important political statement about the evils of nicotine and somehow discourage your guests from smoking on your premises. You will be doing no such thing. You will rather be making an important statement about your insensitivity to people's needs and also be insuring that they will wind up smoking anyway and dumping the ashes into the soil of your delicate begonia plant or grinding them into your rug. A thoughtful host or hostess puts out pretty boxes of matches, too, in places where people can see them.

• To discourage guests from plundering your medicine chest, put out in the bathroom a tiny tray consisting of things they might tend to go scrounging for: aspirin, Band-Aids, and maybe a safety pin or two. A small pot of flowers, such as African violets, makes a bathroom look lovely and cared for and is currently very chic.

• Avoid making friends with people who are able to enjoy your company only after having been fortified with liberal doses of controlled substances. In any case it is never your responsibility to provide these along with the Camembert and crackers. I am probably the last person who should be suggesting how you might deal with people who pull out their own paraphernalia at inopportune times, since most of my friends have jumped on the health bandwagon to the extent that they are even giving up alcohol. But should you wish gently to discourage someone from shocking your visiting great-aunt or a colleague who you hope will provide you with a character reference for your next job, you can probably accomplish that quite easily with a simple "Please —not here."

The rules I've given above apply to almost all large parties, cocktail or otherwise. Now for a few words on some more specialized kinds of parties that have worked well for me or for people I know.

A Wine Shower

Hardly anybody leaves the single lane before having given at least one bridal shower and today men and women are equally likely to be called on to do the honors. A Saturday night wine shower offers a nice way to honor a friend who's getting married but whose household has long since achieved its quota of potato peelers and meat thermometers. Ask each guest to bring a special bottle of wine or an exotic liqueur. (Some people may want to bring an extra bottle so guests can try theirs, too.) A few of you may also want to chip in for a wine rack.

Sunday Brunch

A party that has always worked well for me is Sunday brunch. I usually invite five to ten close female friends. You can entertain more cheaply than you could on Saturday night and might also pull in a few people you wouldn't have the nerve to ask otherwise.

I like to invite guests for twelve noon and to serve a meal somewhere between breakfast and lunch. One favorite menu is scrambled eggs with freshly snipped dill, an assortment of light and dark breads, a cold vegetable salad, and individual fruit tarts or cheesecake for dessert. Another excellent choice is a huge salade niçoise plus whatever French bread is most readily available in your area. Finish off the meal with Maida Heatter's Chocolate Rum Cake or a sumptuous bakery treat.

High Tea

Elegant hotels around the country are reviving the oh, so civilized custom of serving a late afternoon tea. A Sunday afternoon one provides a nice way to entertain friends who rarely return from their beach or ski houses until sometime late in the weekend, and who therefore would be impossible to round up for a Saturday night dinner party.

A classic British tea includes sandwiches made with crustless, thinly sliced white or brown bread, cut into triangles or fingers; fill with sliced cucumber or tomato on buttered bread sprinkled with salt and freshly ground pepper, or with sliced egg or chopped watercress with mayonnaise. You can pick up other ideas in the ten-page section entitled "Canapés and Tea Sandwiches" in the *Joy of Cooking* (Signet, 1973). With the sandwiches, serve fresh scones or crumpets with butter and preserves or even thin slices of fruitcake. An English tea, such as Earl Grey or Queen Mary's, adds to the authenticity. To the party wear a Laura Ashley blouse or a Harris tweed blazer or just a Burberry's scarf thrown casually around your neck. Elizabethan madrigals or something by the early Beatles can set the right musical tone.

Not-So-Trivial Pursuits

A game party makes a nice way to introduce people who don't know each other well. A lot of people plan social events around the popular board game of Trivial Pursuit. It can also be fun to invent your own game of minutia madness, using facts about current news events or the city in which you live. A party of this sort seems to call for dressing down and for serving casual refreshments such as pizza and beer, so note those on the invitation if you're planning to do either.

Sports Spectaculars

Almost any televised sports event can offer a handy excuse to round up a group of friends to watch it on the screen. But two that lend themselves especially well to this purpose are the running of the Kentucky Derby and the unfolding of the Wimbledon tennis championships. Both have been around long enough to have spawned elaborate accompanying festivities, and many can be adapted for use in even a small apartment.

The Kentucky Derby takes only about two minutes to run, on the first Saturday in May, so your guests will have plenty of time for socializing after watching the race on your set. Serve the traditional Derby Day drink, the mint julep. (There's a recipe for it in the *Joy of Cooking* and other comprehensive cookbooks.) All you need in the way of food are some buckets of takeout Kentucky Fried Chicken and whatever you want to serve with them. A bluegrass record on the stereo adds a nice touch, and don't forget to hang on to the preceding day's sports section of the paper, so guests can compare their predictions with those of the experts.

The Wimbledon tennis championships take place in late June and early July, culminating in the men's and women's finals around Independence Day. The spectators at the tournament feast on courtside strawberries and cream. You might combine a Fourth of July barbecue with an Americanized version of the same, such as strawberry shortcake. If the weather permits, move your TV set out onto your terrace so guests can soak up the sun.

Private Screenings

Time was when only the Beverly Hills crowd could catch first-run movies at home. Now almost anybody with a videocassette recorder can do the same—a device that can be especially useful when you're still developing skills as a party-giver. Your guest of honor is the movie you get together to watch, and that puts less strain on you. One woman organized a movie club whose members get together on the first Friday of every month to watch a film chosen at their last meeting. By sharing the cost of a rental or even a purchase, they still wound up paying less than they would by taking in the same fare at Cinema II, where they'd also likely miss the pleasure of each other's company.

Another woman invites people over once a year to watch a tape of *Casablanca*. She always has a few bottles of Vichy water to break out during the final scene and is considering making the event the first leg of an annual Bogart Festival in her home.

Political Fund Raisers

I used to think that fund raisers were mostly for the sort of high rollers who could afford to pay five hundred dollars a plate to eat prime ribs in hotel ballrooms. Today, many successful fund raisers take place in private homes, and almost anybody can give one. Candidates often welcome a chance to attend parties in their honor even when no money is being raised, because it gives them the opportunity to meet prospective voters in a relaxed setting. Call the campaign office of someone you support to find out how you can get in on the action or get in touch with your local Republican or Democratic Committee. If you're interested in giving a party, you may need to come up with your own list of guests (who will be willing to pay anything from five dollars on up to attend). Or maybe the local political party of your choice can help to provide one for you. In any case, you'll address the envelopes and see to the refreshments, and the benefits you get out of it won't be limited to the knowledge that you've helped to do something for your community. Somewhere down the road, the candidate may do something important for you. (Who knows when you may welcome the help of an elected officeholder in getting a variance that would enable your block association to hold a street fair on the premises?) Once you start to give fund raisers for candidates, you may be able to branch out and start arranging them for other sorts of causes, too, such as on behalf of a local park or zoo.

A Loaf of Bread, a Jug of Wine, and Thou . . . and Thou . . . and Thou

Picnics in the park make more than a wonderful way to entertain a date. They also give you a great opportunity to entertain your friends, often less expensively than you could any other way. Nobody minds being asked to bring his or her famous orange-avocado dip to a picnic, so you can sometimes get away with buying almost no food at all.

Picnics also allow you to entertain far more people than you could in a boxy apartment, so you can have bigger celebrations, too. And those get-togethers need not adhere to prescribed rules. It is possible, for instance, to do quite well without any of the traditional alfresco foods, such as fried chicken and potato salad. An impromptu feast might consist of croissants, cold meats and cheeses, and fresh seasonal fruits, all picked up at a takeout shop en route to the riverbank. Julia Child once said that one of her favorite picnic meals consists of cold paella and white wine. I am fond of pita bread pockets stuffed with chopped lettuce and tomatoes, plus cold marinated chicken or beef. Keep the vegetables and meat in tightly sealed plastic containers in a cooler and assemble the pita sandwiches in the park. With them include a few desserts that travel well, such as cherry cream cheese brownies or a small zucchini cake.

A picnic that coincides with a special musical event makes a particularly nice way to bring your friends together. My friend Pam Proctor choreographed annual celebrations in Sheep Meadow, in Central Park, where she and others listened to the New York Philharmonic's "1812 Overture." A Cambridge chum gets her nearest and dearest together every summer to watch the Boston Ballet's performances at the Hatch Shell beside the Charles River.

Another idea is to tap your friends' musical talents. Have one bring a guitar or flute for background music; you provide photocopies of any lyrics people might want to sing.

The rage in my region is for outdoor contra dance parties in a field or large backyard. Contra dancing is a form of English country dancing, similar to square dancing, but more with it. All it requires is that you find a suitable location and hire a caller for a few hours. (To find a contra-dance expert in your area, check the Yellow Pages under "Square Dancing," since many of its callers also work the contra-dance circuit.) Nobody needs any previous experience to get into the swing of things right away, so even your most retiring friends will be quickly drawn into the action.

The Big Sleepover

Remember how much fun it used to be to pile over to somebody else's house, with your sleeping bag in tow, to spend the night eating Fritos and telling ghost stories with friends? It can still be fun to get a small crowd together, to camp out overnight on the floor of your apartment, on a night when none of you has a date. Ask friends to bring a couple of extra blankets if they don't own sleeping bags, so they can bed down comfortably on the floor. You might do this on a night when a popular late movie will be playing on TV or rent one for your VCR. After a single evening of staying up late, talking and drinking wine out of plastic cups, you may feel closer to some of your friends than after months of hastily grabbed hamburgers after work. Sleepovers tend to work best when limited to one sex, but who am I to spoil your fun if you think you can handle a mixed crowd?

The Indoor Cookout

An indoor picnic or cookout sometimes turns out to be the only way you can feed large numbers of people in a small apartment that's scarcely big enough for a buffet table. I got this idea from my friends Tanya Contos and Paul Henry, who once invited guests to a "midwinter cookout" in their Brookline, Massachusetts, home. Though the party was in snowy January, the couple asked people to wear summer clothes. Tanya and Paul then strung up paper lanterns and served foods normally consumed beside a barbecue grill. We didn't roast hot dogs or make s'mores in the fireplace—the main course was a delicious shish kebab—but there's no reason why you *can't.* Let guests eat sitting on the floor, perhaps covered by a picnic blanket or some zany beach towels.

Happy Anniversaries

People who don't have an annual wedding anniversary to celebrate do well to come up with something else to celebrate or commemorate once a year: the opening of the baseball season, the repeal of Prohibition, or the anniversary of Hurricane Carla or the blizzard of '78. A nice idea for someone who never gives a big holiday party in December is to enliven the winter social doldrums by hosting an annual Mozart's birthday party, on or around the anniversary of the composer's birth on January 27, 1756. On the stereo, have "Eine Kleine Nachtmusik" or the album from the Broadway show *A Little Night Music* or from the movie *Amadeus.* Serve traditional Austrian desserts, such as Sacher or Linzer torten. And try especially to have on hand a plate of the chocolate and hazelnut candies known as *Mozart kugeln,* because they were said to have been the composer's favorite. They come wrapped in foil with his picture on each one and are sold in many upscale food stores. *(Mozart kugeln* are also sold by mail order from Paprikas Weiss, 1546 Second Avenue, New York, New York 10028, the catalogue for which costs a dollar.) A more contemporary party might pay homage once a year to Elvis or John Lennon, the latter with all-white napkins and paper plates in honor of the *White Album* or bowls of apples in honor of the Beatles' Apple recording label. The idea is to do a few things to evoke the spirit of any event you honor, but not so many that you get cute or cornball.

An Expatriates' Evening

If you're a transplant to an unfamiliar city, you may be able to take the edge off your homesickness by rounding up a group of people who grew up where you did for dinner parties featuring the foods all of you still like best. Your friends or college alumni/ae association may be able to produce the names of people in your area who fondly remember Maine, California, or New Orleans. Even if they can't, you can still share your favorite foods and customs with others who are meeting them for the first time. Introduce the gang to the cheese-steak sandwiches you loved growing up in Philly or the hush puppies and grits that sustained you in Mobile. A transplanted Houstonian is always threatening to bring several six-packs of Lone Star beer back from her next trip home and to serve them to her friends along with Tex-Mex chili, and she teaches them how to do the Cotton-eye Joe. One of these days *I* am going to give a "Friends of the Big Apple" party for a lot of us in my area who have been uprooted from New York, complete with Coney Island hot dogs and the album from *Forty-second Street.*

A Taste of Beaujolais

Although wine tastings have become a bit old hat, they take on added interest when you give one to introduce people to a particular kind of wine they might be less familiar with. Many people have begun to host tastings of the wine called Beaujolais Nouveau, the first of the Beaujolais wines to be released each year. By French law, the new vintage of this wine is released annually at 12:01 A.M. on November 15, then rushed via Concorde to the United States. Because it is meant to be drunk within six months of its issue, bottles appear almost immediately in liquor stores around the country, amid a flurry of newspaper articles rating the different brands. Among the more popular is Louis Jadot's Beaujolais Villages Nouveau. Round up an armload of different brands or see if you can arrange with a local liquor merchant to have a tasting in your home; some dealers will provide the wine free if you allow them to make a short sales pitch explaining the properties of different kinds. Serve plates of French cheeses, including not just the familiar Brie and Camembert but St. André, Doux de Montagne, Gourmandise, and Montrachet.

A Party for Somebody Else

Nothing can be more fun, or make you feel better about yourself, than giving a gala for someone you love. One advantage of doing so is that, even if the event turns out to be a total fizzle, you needn't worry; you may never need to see your guests again, because they were somebody else's friends and not yours. You may already have given your ration of showers and bachelor parties, so why not come up with some other excuses to honor your kith? Give a surprise birthday or going-away party, or put together a small celebration in honor of someone who's just made partner or gotten an M.B.A.

I often give book-publication parties for friends who are authors. The first such celebration I hosted of this sort took place some years ago, after I learned that a colleague's publisher did not plan to give a similar event. It seemed a terrible injustice that a book that had been so long aborning should come into the world with no fanfare at all. As I considered giving a party, however, two problems presented themselves: the small size of my apartment and my limited knowledge of my colleague's circle of friends. I solved the first by asking a mutual acquaintance whether I might borrow her expansive, terraced penthouse for one evening. Then I asked the author if she would supply a list of friends who might like to attend the party I wanted to give for her. She agreed and later reported that the man she was involved with would be willing to provide the champagne for the event. The result was a lively celebration that justly honored a friend in grand style—and yet they didn't spill out of my postage-stamp-sized apartment or leave me en route to debtor's prison.

Admittedly, giving a party for somebody else can be expensive. You may, however, be able to trim the costs by cohosting a celebration for several others. Besides, can you really expect that someone will someday give you the big party you've always dreamed about if you've never done the same sort of thing for somebody else?

Your Birthday

Before I got up the nerve to give my own birthday parties, I used to rely on the services of my childhood friend, Dennis Frenchman. As I recall, I would call him about something else and then slip in sweetly, "And, oh yes, what are we doing for my birthday two weeks from tomorrow?"

Sometimes I was slightly more subtle. "By the way," I would say, "I thought it might be a nice idea if you gave a little birthday dinner party for your friend Barry." A weighty pause followed. "You know, his birthday is two days before mine, and we could celebrate together."

But why not be cheerily direct? One man, whom I will call Bob Smith, has for some years now been sending invitations to what he bills as "Bob Smith's Annual Twenty-ninth Birthday Party." At this point nobody has any idea how old he really is, and who cares? All Bob's friends know that his parties are legends in their own season, thanks to his daring.

Another nice way to make your birthday memorable is to celebrate it with a friend whose own birthday falls at around the same time. My friend Aimee Ball and I, living as we do in different cities, rarely can be together on both our birthdays, which fall within a month of each other. But we can sometimes manage to be together for one, which becomes a joint celebration for both of us. You might tie your birthday celebration to the nearest holiday, inviting people to "Louisa's Annual Valentine's Day/Birthday Party" or "Steve's Fourth of July Barbecue and Birthday Celebration."

Mark special birthdays such as your thirtieth in an especially interesting way. Have a champagne-and-cake party at your place or in a private room of a restaurant. You could even hire someone to come in to entertain: a baroque trio, a jazz pianist, or a music major at a local college. Or rent a sail or other boat for a few hours on a warm evening and take your friends out for a trip.

At least spread the word about your birthday in whatever way you can. One woman I know did this quite handily by writing in the appropriate box on a wall calendar in her office, "My birthday." A man casually remarked to his friends, a week or two before his birthday arrived, "My birthday is coming up in a week or two, and I'm looking for a special restaurant to try in honor of the occasion. Can you suggest some place out of the ordinary?" As things turned out, Jack's friends didn't take him to the restaurant he'd been looking for, which he wanted to try with a date. But, once alerted to his birthday, they arranged a lovely office party complete with flowers, a cake, a singing birthday-gram delivered by a singing tap dancer dressed up like the Philip Morris boy.

In any case, you are making an emotional kamikaze flight if you always leave it to others to think of ways to celebrate your birthday. Nobody always has a date on his or her big day, and neither can everybody count on having his or her friends around for it without taking steps to insure that they will be. Do it up big, do it up small, but do it up somehow, and rejoice. For as long as you are single, you can give the sort of birthday party you always wanted, and even get the present you always wanted, too, because, after all, you bought it for yourself.

Naturally, you can find other sorts of wonderful parties to give—some occasionally, and others year in and year out. And the best part of doing so might be that, by giving a great party, you've often given much more to the people you know. If you choose your guests carefully, you will have helped your guests find fun, friends, colleagues, and contacts. You've made yet another contribution to the people who contribute so much to your well-being, or one of many small offerings to the world that can add up to a big one.

With any luck, you will soon have as many friends as you can handle. Then your biggest problem won't be how to make more—it will be where to put them all.

6

The User-Friendly
Apartment

A lot of single people believe they can survive happily amid even the rudest surroundings. They insist they don't in the least mind living with mismatched dishes, barren walls, and furniture that anyone weighing more than eighty-five pounds needs to be warned away from. After all, they say, their apartments are simply surrogate offices, or places to shower or shave en route to the theater. Besides, their living quarters are only temporary. The lease will be up soon, and then they can move to someplace nicer. And one day soon they will get married—and have real homes of their own.

These popular views notwithstanding, an apartment can be far more than a place to mark time between school and marriage, or between one marriage and another. Lavish or modest, your home is the focal point for your entire life. Upgrade it and you may improve everything else in the process. Run it into the ground and you may require all the strength you have just to keep from sinking along with it.

Having a comfortable home matters partly because the

place you live in may be the most important thing in your
life that you can largely control. Lovers can leave you; employers can go bankrupt; and friends can get transferred
just when you need them the most. But a place you love will
never abandon you for someone richer or better-looking or
fire you in a company-wide layoff the day after the third-
quarter earnings come in. Like a good friend, it is always
"there" for you, in stormy weather or fair.

A nice home says wonderful things about you to other
people, too. A handy measure of your self-esteem, it tells
the world: "I have gone to the trouble of fixing my place up
because I believe I'm worth it. I deserve a nice home, and I
have one." It's possible to send that message before you
quite believe it—and to begin to believe simply because
other people do.

Beyond that, your home is the place you usually entertain
in, and a lovely one makes you likely to do it that much
more often. So, the better you like your place, the stronger
your honorary family usually becomes. With a home you
love, you won't just have your friends over for an annual
Christmas party so mobbed that nobody will notice that you
don't have curtains on the windows; you'll have them over
often. And your ties to those people are likely to become all
the more significant because you do.

In more than a decade of singlehood, I have lived at a half
dozen addresses in several cities, in structures ranging from
an improbable Tudor high-rise to a garden apartment with
wall-to-wall avocado carpeting in every room. One place,
though beloved, was so small I had to store my ironing
board in the shower and serve my guests dinner on TV
trays. Another was a fifth-floor walk-up on a fire escape, on
which some of my neighbors set up hibachis in summer.
And I remember none without a certain affection and good
will. Each place I lived in let me see myself against a different backdrop that contributed, in its own way, to my
emerging sense of self.

I also learned some lessons from signing my early leases.

The most important is simply that it pays to spend a long time looking for the right apartment, because you inevitably wind up spending a longer time there than you think you will. This caveat especially applies if you live in New York, where good apartments are so hard to find that, once you land one, you may live there practically forever. In fact, if you have your heart set on living in Manhattan or one of the more fashionable sections of Brooklyn, you may well have to resign yourself to months of camping out in a garden apartment in a nearby suburb, until you can find something decent.

Except in New York, though, your biggest temptation will be signing a lease too quickly, even after viewing only two or three places. Two or three months isn't really too much time to invest in looking for an apartment you may inhabit for several years. One way to buy yourself that time is to consider staying for a while at a cozy guesthouse or at a bed-and-breakfast inn. The latter exist even in Manhattan. Check the travel section of any large bookstore for guides to such accommodation in the area you'll be moving to.

Before I moved to Boston, I knew I didn't want to feel pressured into taking an apartment too quickly. So I set aside one day in which to visit every reasonably priced guesthouse within a fifteen-minute subway commute of my new office. (Guesthouses, I found, usually have a separate listing from those of hotels and motels in the Yellow Pages.) I eventually settled into a gracious, half-timbered inn in suburban Brookline that provided me with a large room, plus use of a huge kitchen and solarium, for less than the cost of many apartments. The guesthouse happened to be just down the street from a world-class medical center, so boarders often included visiting doctors from around the world—a fascinating group to run into while broiling a hamburger after work. Staying at the inn for a few months allowed me to try on one community for size while exploring others at night and on weekends. Had I not been able to find such pleasant surroundings at a guesthouse, however, I would also definitely have considered subletting an apartment or two until I found one I wanted to move into for the long term—an option too many single people ignore.

Where to Live

What should you look for in the place you eventually move into? The single most important thing to look for is a safe neighborhood that also attracts lots of your peers. If you need to live in a suburb or small town where the major industry is marriage, try to live either in a group house or in an apartment complex with people who share your age and marital status. You might find a place with kindred spirits by looking for such amenities as a swimming pool, tennis courts, a barbecue pit, game rooms, or a full calendar of social activities for tenants, features which foster a sense of community among residents, too. Places like Sandburg Village, on the Near North Side of Chicago, attract lots of young professionals, married and single, and bring them together with tennis round robins and similar events. Terrific! Singles-only apartment complexes are now against the law in many parts of the country, but you can still find spots that attract unattached men and women by looking for ads that hype their "carefree" or "adult" living.

I know that this idea of trying to live with people who are basically *like* you goes against the popular idea that all of us ought to try to bubble away in one big melting pot that includes everybody. But the conventional wisdom has its flaws. I once lived in an apartment complex that had almost nothing but married people—this at a time when I was feeling especially vulnerable and in need of all the support I could get—and it practically was the end of me. Once you have reached age thirty or so, younger if you live outside a large city, you will have married friends in droves. What you will need to make an extra effort to find are single friends, and you can give yourself a chance to connect with them by carefully choosing the place you call home.

Next to living in a place with lots of people like you, the best alternative is to live in one that your friends can at least get *to*. A handsome, unmarried lawyer of my acquaintance had always wanted to live on the water. So, after law school, when all of his friends were madly signing leases for high-rise apartments in the city, he opted to move into a charming bungalow on the ocean, forty-five minutes outside town by commuter rail. For a fraction of what his friends paid for their cramped plaster boxes in midtown, he had three bedrooms and a vast plate-glass window overlooking the sea. It should have been paradise—and he was absolutely miserable for the entire time he lived there. His nearest neighbor was a half mile away, and even that one only lived there in the summer. After a grueling day in court, the young lawyer could never invite his friends to drop by for a drink, because nobody just drops by a place as far out of town as his was. On dates, he was always either begging out early in order to catch the last train back to his seaside cottage or paying a fortune to garage his car overnight. A single winter in his dream home nearly suffocated his social life before it even got off the ground, and he moved out, not a moment too soon, at the first sign of spring.

Apart from looking for a place in an upbeat neighborhood, I believe you ought to look for two particular amenities in the apartment itself. One is a working fireplace, and the other is a small patch of outdoor space, in the form of a terrace, deck, patio, or small yard.

Have a Hearth

Hearth and home have always been so closely linked that a fireplace has benefits that are as much psychic as aesthetic. After a year of living alone in a house on a remote stretch of the Cape Cod beach, naturalist Henry Beston wrote, in *The Outermost House* (Penguin, 1981), that his fire was "more than a source of heat—it was an elemental presence, a household god, and a friend." Even the split logs stacked up beside my own hearth make me feel good, as though I am connected to a force bigger than I am. A local floral designer made me a huge silk flower arrangement, filled with vivid red amaryllis and orange day lilies to echo the colors of a flame, in a brass pot that fits inside the opening of the fireplace when it's not in use. So, even in summer, my hearth seems to set my entire living room ablaze with color and light.

Much as I love my fireplace, however, I would sacrifice even it for a small patch of outdoor space adjoining my apartment. The mere presence of a door that opens out onto the outside world somehow always seems to make you feel as though you are really living instead of observing life through your window. Like a fire, it connects you to the elements, which is part of what life is all about. You can plant basil or tomato plants and watch them grow. You can sit outside after work and watch the sun set or the snow fall. You can also hang a bird feeder—as I do—and wake up daily to the sight of chickadees and house finches breakfasting on your handout.

All such comforts can, it seems, mean a great deal when you are single. A married person often stays in touch with the unfolding of life simply by watching a child grow. He or she is also more likely than a single one to own a house surrounded by trees, grass, and flowers. In the absence of other ways to stay in touch with the unfolding of life, single people need to pay especially close attention to the cycles of nature or risk feeling cut off from something so primal that it almost can't be put into words. A single, female New Yorker once admitted to me, "The thing I like least about my life right now is how rarely I see a tree that's not growing on a rooftop." Precisely. But how much better to see a tree—or a flower or a sparrow—on a rooftop than not at all. And, if you can't afford the sort of penthouse roof garden that my friend was referring to, you can afford something else that will put you on intimate terms with the local flora and fauna, if you wait long enough.

There are, of course, many other things that it's wonderful to have in an apartment than a fireplace and outdoor space. Should you be a little older or more affluent, try to look for an apartment with what I call great "bones," or architecture so interesting it seems to need almost no decoration. Lots of single people move into places that have nothing more going for them than their price, believing they will quickly be able to cozy them up to look like something out of *House and Garden.* Forget it. In my experience, the department store never delivers the sofa on time; the curtains always take months to get put up; and the idea of painting the walls sky blue or apricot, which seemed so appealing when you first looked at them, loses its appeal the moment you move in and realize the chaos that the project would cause. By the time you complete all your projects, your lease is up, and meanwhile you have spent months or even years always feeling a little dissatisfied with the space you come home to each night. It seems so . . . unfinished.

A better idea is to hold out for a space so great, you can love it from the moment you move in and so will the people who visit you. This sort of place often has one feature so dramatic that nobody ever notices that there are no curtains on the windows or rugs on the floors. A friend once lived in a place with an exposed brick wall running along the length of the living room, which, because the unit was tiny, really meant along the length of the entire apartment. To this day, I couldn't tell you whether her apartment had rugs on the floor or paintings on the wall; all I remember is that fabulous exposed brick. Other people have river views or cathedral ceilings that have a similar effect on visitors. I've lived in my current place for a year and still don't have curtains in the living room or a rug bigger than the one that fits under my coffee table. But I don't *need* them, because I have three fireplaces, french doors opening out onto a wrought-iron balcony with a glittering view of the city skyline at night, and four walls of built-in pine bookcases filled with novels, so who has to have curtains to feel at home there? But I waited, literally, eight months for the place to become available, then snapped it up instantly. And that is what you, too, need to do to find a really wonderful place you can afford. You look and look and look—and then, when you find the apartment you know is in a class by itself, you *pounce*.

His and Her Habitats

After you pounce, of course, you think about decorating, by which I simply mean giving your place a little personality, if not outright pizzazz. How you go about that project will probably have at least a little to do with your sex, because the sexes tend to make different design mistakes, which are worth noting at least briefly.

Single women's apartments often suffer from a severe case of the cutes. It is scarcely possible to turn around in many of them without seeing a mug with a smile on it, a poster listing the number of calories burned up by unprintable sex acts, or a pillow bearing the legend: "In order to meet your prince, you have to kiss a lot of toads." (I always wonder how men feel about posters suggesting that their romantic overtures are little more than a means to work off a slice of Key lime pie and pillows that consign them to virtually certain toadhood before a romance has even begun.) You may also see anemic spider plants, wobbly rattan tables, and pop-art posters. I often believe, in a single woman's apartment, that the whole thing ought to be stamped: "Perishable."

Not that most single men's apartments are likely to look as though the editors of *Architectural Digest* just left, taking their strobe lights and black umbrellas with them. Just as single women's apartments tend to suffer from the cutes, single men's tend to manifest what might be called the bachelor beige syndrome. Everything tends to be done in shades of brown, down to the reproduction oriental rug underfoot. The furniture leaves the impression that a surgeon was called in to graft it onto the premises directly from a showroom in Bloomingdale's. What is missing is usually any trace of the unique personality of the owner, whether in the form of framed family photos, hand-embroidered pillows, or tall plants that somebody has clearly tended.

The homes of both sexes tend to reflect a timidity that stems from inexperience. Many single men and women are furnishing places for the first time and are understandably reluctant to make mistakes. So they err on the side of conformity instead of on the side of originality. Yet their caution often turns out to be a mistake in itself, because what it can leave them with is an apartment that cost a fortune to furnish—and can't be distinguished from anybody else's.

The Pros and Cons of Using a Pro

There *is* a way around the tentativeness that afflicts so many single people's decorating efforts. In fact, there are lots of ways around it. But they don't necessarily conform to what the decorators—or the interior-design magazines— tell you to do.

The pros, for instance, are always telling people to begin their decorating efforts by drawing up little floor plans of their homes on graph paper. Then you are supposed to make scale models of your furniture and push them around on graph paper until everything clicks neatly into place.

It's a pretty funny idea, isn't it? There the decorators are telling you to make these cute little models, when you live in an apartment so small you have a maximum of three possible combinations and could just push all of the furniture around and *see* how it looks with less trouble than it would require to make one of those floor plans, even if you had any graph paper around.

So let's forget, for the moment, about what the pros have to say, and let's look at some practical realities. Foremost among them is that there are essentially five ways of getting the better of any empty apartment before it gets the better of you:

1. Fill your apartment with rented furniture while you figure out what, if any, major pieces you want to own.

2. Hire a decorator to tell you what you want and then get it for you.

3. Hire a decorator to give you a few suggestions and then execute them on your own.

4. Furnish your apartment yourself with hefty servings of advice from your friends and others.

5. Furnish your apartment without getting help from anybody at all, a decorating style that might be called Early Winging It.

Renting furniture for a few months is—surprise—not always to be ruled out. Leasing some big pieces for a while may allow you to save up for the first-rate ones you want instead of settling for the second-rate ones you can afford at the time you move in. Renting furniture can also be a necessity when you are forced to relocate suddenly and have arrived in town before your Breuer chairs. Most large cities have one or more companies that provide this service, listed in the Yellow Pages under "Furniture Renting and Leasing," and many will deliver as much as you need with less than a week's notice. As little as a hundred dollars or so a month may get you all the pieces you need to fill up a living room and bedroom, including lamps and other accessories. Some nurseries and plant stores will even rent you the greenery you need to add a little life to the picture. Most furniture leasing companies offer rent-with-option-to-buy plans that allow you to apply part of your fee toward the purchase of any items you decide you can't live without.

Hiring a decorator can also make sense, especially when you have lots of money at your disposal—and a willingness to spend six months to a year or longer waiting for the project to come together. A decorator usually obtains furniture and other items at wholesale prices, typically forty percent or more off retail, then adds a commission of twenty percent or more that brings the cost of the pieces back up. But such pros can be infinitely worth their price tag, for at least four reasons:

1. Decorators will come up with ideas far more imaginative than you could think up on your own, resulting in a look far more breathtaking than you could achieve alone.

2. Decorators can spare you costly mistakes, because they know what won't work along with what will.

3. Decorators have access to stores that sell "to the trade only," meaning to architects and designers exclusively, which offer things you couldn't buy retail.

4. Decorators can be a godsend for people who have no time to shop, because they will do virtually everything for you, right down to bringing fabric swatches to your office, if needed.

Best of all, you don't have to hire a decorator to do your entire apartment. Although most of them still work exclusively on a commission basis, an increasing number will sell you advice at an hourly rate.

How can you find a decorator whose tastes are compatible with yours? The experts tell you to find friends whose places you admire—and then ask for the names of the decorators who did them. Most of my friends, though, would sooner have butlers or valets. So you might instead seek leads on the home furnishings pages of your local paper or call to see if the local chapter of the American Society of Interior Designers publishes a list of its members. Another good idea is to visit the annual "show house" of decorators' efforts sponsored in many communities by the Junior League or another organization. If all else fails, be brazen. I found one terrific designer when a realtor showed me an apartment that, although not right for me, had nonetheless been decorated to within a hair's breadth of my tastes. I jotted down the name of the tenant off the buzzer, then wrote him a short note requesting the name of his designer and enclosing a stamped, self-addressed envelope. The designer's name I sought came back by mail almost immediately and is filed in my wish book.

You may also be able to find a designer simply by walking into the home furnishings department of any large department store. Bloomingdale's, for instance, has a staff of pros who will provide complete design services, including visiting customers' homes. Top-of-the-line furniture stores often offer the same sort of assistance. Many single people turn to the design pros at Roche Bobois, which tends toward a sophisticated, contemporary look, found in its stores nationwide.

If you decide to use a decorator who takes a commission on furnishings sold to you, be up front about money. Some designers who work on commission require that you spend a minimum amount per room. Find out right away if yours does. It's almost always possible to find a decorator who'll work within a tight budget, if you say clearly what it is and are willing to shop around to find someone who'll work within it.

How To Be Your Own Decorator

A few words, at last, on doing your own decorating, beginning with one caveat: most of us who are single just don't have the taste, the experience, or the judgment to be able to do everything right the first time we fix up a place. So don't even try. Swallow your pride and solicit suggestions from all the people whose taste you admire: your friends, your dates, your parents, or somebody who lives in your building and whose apartment has the same layout as yours . . . but somehow looks so much more fantastic. Money may not make as much of a difference as you imagine; some people just have a better eye for line, color, and proportion than others. Avail yourself of the expertise of your decorating betters. Not many people will take offense if you say: "My place is very small, and I couldn't begin to furnish it nearly so beautifully as yours, but I would be so grateful if you'd be willing to drop by my place one day and give me a few pointers on where to put my pictures and how to arrange the furniture."

Until you can get up the gumption to ask for help, try at least to take copious notes on other people's places. I used to carry a small notebook around to the dinner parties I attended at the homes of wealthy older friends. The moment the host or hostess went out in the kitchen to flambé the bananas or mince the fresh coriander, I would frantically begin drawing little sketches of the arrangements of bibelots on a mantel or prints on a wall. (Were the prints hung asymmetrically or at right angles? Were the larger ones on top or on bottom, and in the center of the arrangement or on the outside?) Sometimes the host or hostess never went out to the kitchen at all, and I would be forced to lock myself into the bathroom while I scribbled impressions of what I'd seen—the color of the rug in relation to the color of the sofa, and that sort of thing. All of this helped to sharpen my eye for scale and detail in a way that merely browsing in stores never could have, because stores never do things the way you would at home, where you have to contend with odd angles and stray objects that they never have in the Crate & Barrel showroom.

Once you're ready to start decorating instead of just listening and observing, begin with your biggest items and work down to the smaller ones. First take care of your walls and floors, then get your sofa. This point is vital, because the biggest mistake single people make in fixing up their apartments is to buy a sofa first and then to try to do the rest of a room around it, which is a little like buying a shirt and then looking for a suit to go with it. Not many living-room couches have the clout to carry an entire room by themselves or even to help unify it. Yet they can lock you into a color scheme nonetheless. Their fabrics and designs also tend to date and wear out quickly, often before you have finished pulling the rest of the room together. A sofa, finally, tends to need at least two coordinating chairs to go with it, so people can sit across from each other and talk. But you may not be willing or able to afford to buy all of those together before you have some idea of how the rest of the room will shape up.

Try especially to get your landlord to paint before you move in, and not just because you will have a real mess on your hands if you decide to have the job done afterward. A fresh paint job also helps to seal off access routes for cockroaches. All of those tiny little cracks and crevices, around doorjambs and floorboards, make ideal spaces for household pests to squeeze in through. A couple of coats of paint can eliminate many of them before you move in and thereby save you a fortune on Black Flag roach spray later. (If you see bugs on your initial inspection, insist that your landlord call in an exterminator before you move in, or bring in one yourself.) If your landlord won't paint, you may be able to hire a couple of college students to do the job for you for far less than a pro would charge.

Then give some thought to your floors. Beautifully finished hardwoods are every tenant's dream. Badly scarred ones are a form of urban blight unto themselves. If yours fall into the latter category, see if your landlord will redo them or allow you to get them done and deduct the cost from your rent. You might also consider sprucing them up yourself, either with wax or one of the popular polyurethane finishes. If your floors are so badly damaged that neither you nor anybody else wants the thankless task of redoing them, see if you can obtain your landlord's permission to cover them with a couple of gallons of crisp white deck paint from a marine supply store. The effect can really be quite spiffy, especially when you add some brightly colored furniture and lots of greenery to jazz things up.

Then you'll probably also need something with which to cover your floors. I'd plump for the best-quality oriental rug you can afford. I'd do that at least partly because a good one is singularly adaptable. A Persian carpet that graces a living room today can work just as well in a bedroom or den next year. It will also show dirt far less readily than anything else you can buy and is therefore ideal for an apartment shared with roommates or with lots of guests trooping in and out. Most of all, though, an excellent oriental gives you a color scheme strong and rich enough to help unify the entire rest of a room and thereby gives you a head start on creating a place that you'll love. You can pick up one of its primary colors for your sofa, a secondary one in an armchair. You can move to a new apartment in which none of your furniture works but still use the same rug as the ground of an entirely new grouping. One unmarried couple grew so attached to the oriental rug that had followed them to three apartments that they unrolled it in the meadow in which they eventually had a wedding ceremony, with folding chairs set up on it instead of on the grass.

Many single people avoid orientals because they think of them as dark and dreary or just a little too staid. That isn't always true. Two other kinds of rugs that nevertheless have a fresh, youthful look are *kilims* and *dhurries,* both of them lightweight flat weaves that have lately come into popularity. Unlike some Persian rugs, kilims and dhurries can usually be rolled up and stored or moved easily, making them wonderful for especially nomadic single people. Dhurries, made in India, come in a variety of patterns, including floral and geometric motifs. Kilims, often from Turkey or Romania, tend to have bold designs in shades of rust, gray brown, or black. Of course, many other kinds of rugs can work equally well (though I'm ruling out wall-to-wall carpeting as simply too impractical). American Indian rugs, particularly Navajo weaves, can look terrific in contemporary apartments and can also be hung on walls.

If you can't afford a large rug, try to pick up a three-by-five or four-by-six one to go under your coffee table. Even a small rug of this sort can help to give a room a finished look. Put a small Persian or dhurrie under a glass-topped coffee table for an especially nice arrangement. (A cheaper way to achieve the same effect is to have a glass store cut you a piece the size of a coffee table top, then place it on top of bricks or other supports.) A small American hooked or braided rug goes well with a roughly hewn pine or oak table topped with a basket of apples.

So long as you use your rug to provide a color scheme for your room, you almost can't go wrong in decorating it, because you'll always have at least one substantial item tying the whole thing together. But what if you can't afford a nice one, or just have floors that seem somehow too beautiful to cover up? Then you might find a very large print or painting that you like and derive a color scheme from it. Another idea is to be guided by the colors of a bouquet of silk flowers, a needlepoint sampler, or a folding screen behind which you hide your bicycle. Any of these will usually have a color scheme far richer than you could find in a sofa and that therefore will hold up better over the long haul.

Whatever colors you choose, make sure every room you fix up has a clearly defined focal point—a single spot to which your eye is inevitably drawn. A fireplace provides a natural one, but even it needs to be played up. Place two love seats opposite each other in front of it, or give the same spot to a small sofa across from two chairs. If you don't have a fireplace, try to give the room some cohesion by playing up something else, such as a terrific view or an interesting built-in arrangement. Don't scatter your furniture all about the room; group it in such a way that it enhances the room's best feature. Do you have a totally plain room devoid of any redeeming features? Buy one huge, terrific print and plan everything else around it.

What else do you need to make a place come to life? Almost nothing makes you feel so adult as owning a good, big bed, instead of a convertible sofa or mattress on the floor. Buying a real desk is a wonderful rite of passage; there's nothing like not having to pay your bills at the same table at which you spoon banana-apple yogurt out of the container. But if you can't afford a desk *and* a table, consider a round table approximately thirty-six inches in diameter. These are more versatile than almost any you can name and will last forever. Long after it has grown badly scarred from years of constant use, a round table will still serve you handily when covered with a beautiful floor-length cloth. It can be your primary space for eating and working when you are starting out, then be transformed into an accessory in a bedroom or living room. A round table acquires instant chic when you top it with a floor-length skirt or tablecloth, then put a brass-pot lamp on top of that, and cluster plants and photos around it. A gateleg or other drop-leaf table makes another great investment. Display it opened up when you haven't got much furniture and push it closed up against a wall once you've acquired more. Don't even *consider* blowing your savings on a dining-room table until you've at last found your dream apartment or house. Meanwhile, you can feed lots of people at a sit-down dinner, more inexpensively, by buying a folding aluminum picnic table that costs less than fifty dollars. Cover it with a floor-length or other tablecloth—and nobody will know that somebody's Chippendale treasure doesn't lie underneath. A classic butler's table, in a beautiful wood such as mahogany or walnut, makes an ideal incidental table for a living room or study.

Then you may also need some lamps, because the light in many city apartments is fit only for trolls. I sought for years to brighten up dim apartments by using standard lighting fixtures and found that none quite did the trick. I've since discovered lamps with what is called a "mogul" socket. These lamps can accommodate a 300-watt bulb that is often surrounded by several other sockets for 60- or 100-watt bulbs, for as much as 700 watts in all. Do get one if you feel as though you are living in a cave.

Antiques for Agnostics

Decorating gets to be really fun once you've acquired most of the things you need and can start picking up a few luxuries, perhaps even an antique or two. When should you begin to start investing in these?

I used to think that, to be able to afford antiques, you had to be practically an antique yourself. Besides, the few old furniture pieces that I owned were old and ratty, not old and ravishing, and they represented precisely what I wanted to move away *from*.

Even so, I wish now that I had at least started to venture into antique stores in my twenties, when the low prices of many items might have surprised me even more than they do today. What I hadn't realized was simply this: most such stores sell far more than rare Federal-period treasures. Furniture experts define an "antique" as anything one hundred years or more old, and a "semi-antique" as something fifty to a hundred years old. The buys in the latter category often represent much better deals than you could get on something new, both because they are more interesting to look at and because they tend to have been made better. Spend a few hundred dollars on a contemporary living-room sofa and you will be hard put to come up with a piece that looks anything but hackneyed. Spend the same amount of money on a carved Victorian-style love seat, made during the 1930s, and you may have an item to cherish for a lifetime and pass on to your heirs. (Add a Victorian rocker and a Boston fern perched high on a stand and maybe a framed nineteenth-century bookplate—and you have an instant Victorian room, while everybody else is practically drowning in smudged white chipboard and badly scratched-up chrome.) I'm not sure I'd ever buy another contemporary piece without at least looking to see what might be available for the same price at an antique store, flea market, or auction.

You can find especially good buys on all sorts of old things at estate sales in which the entire contents of a decedent's house are sold off at once. Many are staged by the grieving relatives of someone who has just died, often people who have flown into town for only a few days and just want to get the whole thing over with. Get to an estate sale early to try to get a leg up on the professional dealers, who hope to snare the rare finds. Show a lot of enthusiasm for anything you want to buy and you may be that much ahead of the game, so moved will the sellers be by your love for Great-aunt Penelope's favorite mahogany credenza. Forget the listed or asked prices and make outrageously low offers on anything that interests you. These sales, once again, must often be completed in one day. So, if your offer isn't accepted immediately, you may want to leave and return late in the afternoon to see if the sellers are willing to come down in price.

How can you know which antiques will escalate dramatically in value? As a beginner, you can't! It takes years to be able to spot that rare Eastlake dresser, in mint condition, that somehow even the dealers overlooked. It can take a lot of time even to be able to tell an original Tiffany lamp from one of its hordes of imitators. So buy simply what you love and know that you will continue to cherish for years. Look especially at the basic lines of a piece. A good refinisher or upholsterer can work wonders with surface damage. (And, since what you're buying represents less a financial investment than an aesthetic one, you don't need to worry about whether such cosmetic changes will decrease its value, as you would if you were a pro.) Yet, if superficial tears and scratches usually can be fixed, grace and beauty of line and proportion can never be added to a piece. They have to be there from the start. So try to train your eye to recognize these by visiting the furniture galleries at museums. Start, the next time you're in Manhattan, by visiting the New England furniture gallery at the Metropolitan Museum of Art. Although small, this gallery contains many exquisite styles and pieces that have been widely copied over the past two centuries and that can quickly give you a sense of how to tell the real thing from a clone.

A reasonable goal, even when you're in your early twenties, is to be able to buy one really good piece a year, preferably an antique or semi-antique. By "good" I mean something that you know will last you for a lifetime and you know you will never want to part with. You might buy this item each year around your birthday as your present to yourself. In any case, it needn't cost a mint. A hundred dollars or less can bring you an art nouveau mirror, a set of lead crystal glasses, a framed copperplate engraving, some antique needlepoint pillows, a beautifully carved side chair, or some Fiestaware pottery pieces that mark the beginning of a collection. Spend a little more, up to two hundred and fifty dollars or so, and you may find a Victorian rocker; a small Amish quilt, in crib or twin size; four chairs to go around a table; or a funky old dictionary stand that gives any room pizzazz. The idea is to make sure you find something that you love so much it raises any room to a higher power. Part of what makes being single occasionally so tough is the feeling that nothing in your life seems to last from one year to the next (which is, of course, precisely what prompts a lot of people to get married). But there are many ways to start giving your life a little durability, and one can be simply by choosing your furnishings with an eye toward their permanence.

Finishing Touches

Finally, a few words on the amenities that can help pull everything else together:

Flowers: Nothing gives a room a lift so quickly and easily as flowers, and never mind that they can cost only slightly less than a late-model Porsche. The best way to be able to afford them is to remember that, the commoner the species, the more of it you generally need to make it look good. The familiar carnations and daisies, for instance, may be the least expensive flowers you can buy, while orchids cost far more. But an entire bouquet of carnations or daisies carries less dramatic impact than a single cymbidium orchid in a vase by itself, which may thus turn out to be more cost-effective in the long run. If you need lots of blossoms for a party or similar event remember that a mixed bouquet often carries less clout than a bunch of one species alone or of several in the same color. I often buy lots of white flowers, such as white freesias or narcissus, and arrange them throughout my apartment before guests turn up on the scene. I like to put them out in the round glass vases that are so popular now, because these can hold seashells or chocolate kisses after the blooms fade.

Books: An apartment with built-in bookcases is always a real find, and, after the fireplace and the outdoor space, they are the first things I look for. Built-ins make books seem like part of the architecture of your life. If you need to house your volumes elsewhere, forget the brick-and-board contraptions that did so well by your Norton anthologies in college. Any grown-up ought to be able to figure out that toting all of them around, every time you move, is going to land you nowhere but in a hernia ward. Buy some commodious bookcases in a nontrendy wood such as oak or walnut. (All of that white chipboard that looks so great in the showroom will be a wreck in a year or two of constant use.) You need bookcases at least twelve inches deep because the shallower ones, of the sort designed for paperbacks, won't hold many of the other things you may want to store on their shelves as well: plants, photographs, and your unread Sunday paper. Another idea is to have a carpenter make you some rectangular cubes approximately $30 \times 15 \times 15$ inches. Have them painted with glossy enamel, so they won't smudge up easily, or get them stained with a deep, rich finish. Because you can stack the cubes many ways, they will easily make the transition from one apartment to the next. Two tall, vertical stacks quickly reassemble into a low-slung horizontal one that fits better in your new place. You can lay a sheet of plywood, stained or painted to match, across the top to form a table or desk. Long after you've finally moved into the house you long to own, your cubes will still be able to hold garden tools or paint cans in the basement.

Original Art: Sooner or later you'll want something on your walls besides the same prints and exhibition posters you see in every apartment on your block. What most single people don't realize is that for the same price you can often buy something far more original that will wear out its welcome far less quickly. The best bets for your money include old maps, bookplates, and prints that you can buy from antiquarian booksellers such as New York's Argosy Book Shop, or at flea markets. Look especially for multiples of prints with a similar theme. Six semi-antique botanical prints, from the pages of a book, can often be had for less money than you'd pay for a single unframed contemporary poster with less artistic wallop. Those same six prints, when beautifully framed, can give a room an instant focal point. If you're unsure of your tastes in art, you can still avoid making mistakes by sticking to representational works of scenes with meaning for you.

The more money you spend for art, however, the more important it is to try to buy only signed and numbered works by artists you like. This helps to insure that you will always buy items of quality, in whatever medium you choose. Try also to learn to recognize the differences between the many kinds of works that are affordable for you now, such as lithographs, serigraphs, intaglio prints, and copperplate engravings. A gallery owner might explain some of these on a slow day when no one else is in the shop.

Tall Trees and Plants: Nobody has ever made a strong case for bringing yet another spider plant into the world, let alone into your apartment. And that's only *one* of the many forms of greenery that have become living, breathing clichés in the homes of single people. Why not at least try to be a little more original? You will get more mileage for your decorating dollar when you buy things, including plants, that you won't see in sixty windows on your street. Among your best bets are trees, or at least huge plants, a minimum of four feet tall. Unlike itty-bitty plants, which tend to drag a room down, towering ones generally tend to lift it up. Often they can substitute for a piece of furniture, though they cost less.

Curiously enough, plants and trees also are a little like children: the bigger they get, the less attention they need. A hired gun could not kill many of the tougher varieties of plants that grow to towering heights, including corn plants, dracaenas, dieffenbachias, and snake plants. I have a four-foot-tall schefflera that I once put into an unused storage room and promptly forgot about. Two months later, when I remembered it, the plant was still going strong—after not having been watered once during that time. Ask your local plant dealer to suggest other species that thrive on neglect.

Ficus trees are finicky but so lush and lovely I think they are worth it. What they mostly need is lots of light plus having their soil soaked with water once a week. (Overwatering can kill one of these beauties as quickly as too little sun.) I have two huge *Ficus benjamina* trees that are practically my adopted children. One is eight feet tall and seems to grow in a hundred directions at once. Last Christmas I threaded tiny white lights among its branches and hung ornaments on them. After the holidays, the ornaments came down and the lights stayed up to give a romantic, almost magical glow to my living room on nights when dates turn up. My other ficus has a braided trunk that constitutes a miracle of horticultural engineering. A small, gold mesh heart—a gift from a loved one—hangs on a branch of the latter and adds a touch of romance and whimsy to my living room.

A Whiff of Something Wonderful: Nothing makes you feel more at home than walking into an apartment in which you smell cinnamon-raisin bread baking in the oven . . . or coq au vin simmering in a Dutch oven on a stove top . . . or a rush of cool air through windows thrown open to a spring breeze. By all means, have any of these if you can— and other wonderful smells, too. Never mind that you live alone. You can still come home from work to smell a rich spaghetti sauce tinged with basil if you fill a slow cooker before leaving in the morning . . . or celebrate the arrival of April with a hyacinth blossom on a tabletop . . . or wake up to the smell of coffee if you invest in a machine that will brew it while you sleep. For the ultimate in aphrodisiacs, take your sheets and pillowcases with you the next time you go out to the country and hang them on a clothesline or tree where they can billow in the clean air—a sure route to sweet dreams for one . . . or two.

But enough about what to put into your apartment. Now a few words about what you should be putting into *you* in order to get what you want out of life.

7

Feeding Yourself

A few years ago, when I told friends that I had received an assignment to write an article about single people and food, I found that almost no one initially took me seriously. One woman asked whether my article would include a sidebar on how to make your own penicillin from the mold growing on your leftovers. Others reminded me of all the jokes about food that the not yet married Rhoda Morgenstern used to crack on the old "Mary Tyler Moore Show." (Sample: "I don't know why I even bother to eat this piece of candy. I should just apply it directly to my hips.") And still other single people simply began to laugh. "Ha-ha," one unmarried friend said. "Single people and food—*that's* a good one." What, I inquired innocently, was so amusing? "I don't know," my friend admitted, starting to laugh again. "It's just . . . funny."

Well, that depends on your perspective. As I began to research the eating habits of single people, I found that there was indeed a comic side to my subject. But whether or not a gastroenterologist would have agreed with me was another matter. My single female friends' refrigerators generally contained so little food as to suggest that they were all being fed intravenously. My single male friends' refrigerators suggested that they were all running imported-beer distributorships. Members of both sexes insisted they would eat better after they got married—and this included people who hadn't even had a date since the first anniversary of the Watergate break-in. In the kitchen, as elsewhere, single people temporized.

Why don't unattached men and women eat better than they do? Here are some of the reasons commonly expressed by single people.

REASON 1: *You don't know how to cook.*

Maybe you've spent your whole life being cooked for by somebody else: your mother, your ex-, or the university dining-hall staff. Can you really be faulted for not knowing how to cook for yourself?

Yes! Anybody who can read a college catalogue can read a cookbook, and somebody who can operate a blow dryer can also learn to wield a blender or boning knife in short order.

Most single people only *think* they can't cook, partly because a lot of the recipes they look at seem too much trouble to bother with. One of my first official purchases as a single woman was a fat, family cookbook of the sort you get for ninety-nine cents, plus three other books and a tote bag, from a book club I had just joined. It seems I was paralyzed with fear that I would one day suddenly be called on to roast a twenty-six-pound turkey or to make a foolproof hollandaise sauce, and I believed neither of these would be possible without a volume as big as the Manhattan phone book to guide me.

Well, not only have I never been called upon to roast a behemoth turkey or make hollandaise sauce for anybody; I also had my taste buds nearly killed by that cookbook, filled as it was with color photographs of things like slithery canned-fruit-and-gelatine desserts that wobbled on the plate. Thankfully, I soon figured out that, while slithery rainbow desserts are fine for church suppers, they are probably not what you want to fix for yourself after a long day at the office or even when a date drops by for a sexy little dinner for two.

That cookbook, though, still taught me an important lesson. The trick when you are just beginning to cook is to look for recipes for things you'll really eat—and also to keep things simple. If you're still living off canned soup and sandwiches, forget trying to make beef Wellington for six. Just learn to make *better* sandwiches, such as Reubens or croque-monsieurs, and work your way up from there. (Either of those can be served to a crowd as successfully as to one or two.) My hefty cookbook got me nowhere, because I didn't want to make Vienna-sausage-and-cornflake casseroles for one or two, let alone for six or eight, the number its recipes inevitably seemed to feed.

I finally got the guidance I needed from the paperback edition of the classic *Joy of Cooking,* which continues to serve me faithfully to this day, along with several others. This perennial favorite leads you by a firm but gentle hand through recipes for almost everything you could want to make, for yourself or somebody else. Two other good bets for culinary agnostics are *Craig Claiborne's Kitchen Primer* (Vintage, 1972) and *The New York Times 60-Minute Gourmet* (Times Books, 1979), by Pierre Franey, with an introduction by Craig Claiborne. Both are filled with recipes as sophisticated as they are simple. My favorite cookbook for single people is *Fearless Cooking for One* (Pocket Books, 1983), by Michele Evans. This is the only volume of its genre that seems to be filled with recipes for the things single people really eat. (Sections have such titles as "Fourteen Chicken Breast Entrees," "One Dozen Hamburgers," and "Fifteen Omelette Recipes.") Its ideas also have an easy grace and intelligence that extend to including suggested appetizers and desserts to accompany main courses.

Naturally, you can also crib a lot of recipes from your

friends or from the cooking classes you take on Saturday mornings. Either of these approaches has the advantage of giving you some idea of how a dish is supposed to turn out. If I could take only one kind of cooking class, I would study not French but Chinese cuisine, because it tends to be simpler and healthier.

Probably the most important thing I ever did for my own cooking, though, was to sit down with my Hungarian grandmother and transcribe all of our family recipes that had previously existed nowhere but in her head. If you have such a relative, you need actively to interview her for all of the instructions that exist only in her head—and should your subject not be around in ten or twenty years, you will never stop being grateful, as I am, that you did so while you could.

REASON 2: *Even if you knew how to cook, you don't have time to do it.*

Translated, this usually means: "I'm too tired to cook when I get home from work. Besides, I haven't got any food in the house, anyway, because on Saturday, when other people were shopping, I was riding a chair lift in Killington." Common as it is, this argument tends to be based on the idea that cooking somehow has to be a big "project." What most single people don't realize is how many dishes can be prepared from scratch more quickly than frozen foods can be heated up in a pouch. Most Chinese stir-fried dishes, for instance, can be whipped up in two or three minutes, or far less than the time it can take to heat up a dinner that's just come out of the freezer. What takes time is mostly the chopping of the food that goes into such meals, something that can often be done in advance. (Slice up your beef or chicken strips for stir frying whenever you buy them, then put them in the freezer; on the day you're ready to use them, just take them out in the morning before you leave for work.) Stir-fry cooking has the added advantage of requiring mostly fresh ingredients and being versatile enough to allow you to prepare almost anything this way. You can stop at a salad bar on your way home from work and pick up all the usual fixings, such as already prepared broccoli, mushrooms, and cauliflower. Then, instead of having them raw, lightly stir-fry them when you get home, either by themselves or with meat or seafood.

In trying to upgrade my own cooking, I have also learned to look for recipes featuring veal scallops, which generally require only a minute or two of sautéing per side. And I have learned to use fresh pasta instead of dried, not just because it tastes better but also because it cooks more quickly, generally in one or two minutes after being dropped into boiling water. Make a tomato sauce for your pasta on weekends, then refrigerate until needed.

Another good idea is to buy a crock pot and a cookbook to go with it. You can pile some meat and vegetables into a crock pot at 8 A.M. and have a juicy stew waiting for you at seven at night. Better still, assemble your stew the night before, heaping the meat and vegetables into the pot before you go to bed. (In the morning, you may be too tired to find your way around the vegetable bin.) When you get up, put your ready-made stew in the refrigerator. Then just reheat after you get home at night.

Finally, if you never cook because you never have the right ingredients on hand after work, keep a small paperback cookbook in your desk at the office or in your attaché case. A good bet for this purpose is Craig Claiborne's aforementioned *Kitchen Primer*. Go over some possible dinner recipes in your lunch hour or take the cookbook with you to the supermarket, should you be the sort of person who never knows what he or she wants to eat until landing in the A & P.

REASON 3: *Even if you knew how to cook and had the time to do it, food has become so expensive that it can be cheaper to eat out.*

Sometimes, alas, this seems to be true. But cooking for yourself isn't just a matter of economy or the lack of it. It's also a way to start living as you'd like to if you were married. You don't, after all, fantasize about getting married only to go out with your spouse to Taco Bell every night. You dream about coming home to the smell of pot roast wafting from the stove or sitting down at a table with flowers and wine goblets on it. So, to stop envying a lot of your married friends, you've got to be able to fix a sexy meal for yourself.

If you chronically eat out or standing up in front of the refrigerator, start small. Don't try to make a five-course meal at once. Bring home your usual half barbecued chicken plucked off a rotisserie, but make a wonderful salad to go with it, with dressing made from scratch instead of poured from a bottle. *I* would have scurvy if it weren't for Rebecca's, a Boston take-out food store that supplements my own culinary efforts.

If money really is an issue, forget about most meat dishes and sidle up to lots of egg and pasta dishes. Of course, to make cut-rate meals such as scrambled eggs so appealing, you've got to do them perfectly. No eggs dumped in a frying pan and then scorched over high heat; they've got to be cooked gently. And you also need to work at perfecting your hamburgers and omelets or wind up feeling defeated even by them.

Another way to beat the high cost of shopping for food is simply to join a food co-op. Most large cities have one or more groups of people who have banded together to buy their food in bulk quantities that are then divided up among members. The majority of the people in these co-ops seem to be—you guessed it—single. So joining one may give a boost to your social life even as it remedies the somewhat pathetic state of affairs in your refrigerator.

I have also heard of informal groups of single people who get together one night a month or week, on the same day, for a potluck meal to which everybody contributes a drink. Great! One such group grew so popular and large that it could no longer fit in members' apartments. Its participants

asked a local minister if they could use a large room in the
church basement in return for a dollar-per-person contribution. You may already belong to a church or young adult
group whose members could include regular meals together as part of their social calendar.

REASON 4: *You don't like cooking for yourself because
then you have to eat alone.*

Eating alone—let's face it—will probably never top anybody's list of The Ten Things I Like Most About Being
Single. I am always amazed to read articles that tell single
people to do things such as fixing beautiful five-course meals
for themselves and then eating alone by candlelight. The
one time *I* tried eating alone by candlelight, I felt I was
attending a séance at which I ought to be communicating
with the ghost of Great-uncle Harvey, who might at any
moment begin knocking on the butcher-block table.

Nothing has ever convinced me that I like eating alone
better than I would like eating with a partner, and I'm not
sure I ever will. But having a varied, balanced diet enables
me to enjoy it more than I did before. So does giving myself
permission to leave the dishes in the sink or watch TV while
eating, things I might not be able to do as easily if I were
married. A small television set that fits on my kitchen
counter also lets me watch Peter Jennings while I julienne
the carrots or stem the spinach, not a bad way at all to
unwind after a heavy day at the office.

REASON 5: *You don't want to cook because you will eat
more if you do and then have to worry even more about
your weight than you do now.*

Then why not *lose* the weight once and for all, so that you
can start enjoying one of the major pleasures life and singlehood have to offer? Most people seem to be deterred
from serious dieting by published 1200-calorie-a-day diets
that leave most of us ready to faint at the end of the first day.
What most people fail to take into account is that you don't

have to eat so few calories to lose weight. All you have to do is to eat fewer than the number you are consuming now, which may be more than you think. A relatively inactive person, for instance, needs to consume only 10 calories a day per pound of body weight in order to maintain his or her weight. A moderately active person needs to consume only 15 calories per pound. So a 120-pound engineer, who gets no exercise and spends the entire day punching a calculator at a desk, needs to consume only 1200 calories a day to maintain his or her weight. If you weigh more than that, you're consuming a lot more calories and ought to be able to lose by cutting back a little at a time.

I once lost weight without dieting simply by writing down every calorie I ate in Jan Ferris Koltun's terrific *Eat and Run Diary* (Holt, Rinehart, & Winston, 1985). Once I saw how many calories I was taking in each day, it became very easy to make painless substitutions that gradually left me thinner. Diet margarine had half the calories of regular, diet salad dressing half the calories of the standard bottle kinds. There are even diet pizzas made by Weight Watchers that let me eat my favorite food to my heart's content.

More than that, counting calories has become easier than ever now that most foods sold commercially have their complete nutritional contents on the back. And many of the new low-calorie foods taste better than the varieties that used to be available. Among the best are the tasty Light & Elegant entrees, not just because they are lower in calories than many other so-called "diet" foods but also because they taste the best. Lean Cuisine, Weight Watchers and Mrs. Paul's also make excellent entrees that clock in at about 300 calories apiece. A lot of these entrees are far more satisfying than many fast foods. A Burger King Whopper with Cheese, for instance, has 740 calories, and a Coke adds another 95. For the same number of calories, you could have more than *three* Lean Cuisine entrees, plus a Tab and a salad with diet dressing!

Don't allow yourself to be stymied by the belief that you

can't count calories just because you eat out a lot or can't find your favorite foods in a calorie counter. You'll gradually develop a feel for how many you're taking in regardless. Not many calorie counters, for instance, list the number in a single croissant. But you can find a listing for the same on the back of a box of Pepperidge Farm croissants of about the size you can buy from a bakery.

If you don't want to wind up starved at the end of every day, try to cut back by the week instead of by the day. If you're eating 2200 calories a day now, try to get back to 1750, and don't lose sleep if you don't make it every day. Just try to work it out so that your weekly average comes to 1750 per day. If you're seriously dieting, of course, you may want to go for broke and aim for the often-recommended 1200 calories a day. A lot of professional models bring down their weekly averages by fasting one day a week, not a bad idea if you can swing it.

Eating Out Alone

Once you've begun to do a lot of the above—or otherwise to feel satisfied with what you put into you at home alone— you may still have a hard time eating out by yourself. After all, when you're home, you don't feel conspicuous by your singleness to anybody but yourself. In a restaurant you may well feel like the Lone Ranger. Can eating out by yourself ever be pleasant when you go anywhere besides your corner coffee shop?

The answer is a qualified yes. Lots of single people say they feel that headwaiters treat them like social outcasts— an experience that grows less common every year. If you fear the cold shoulder, however, it generally makes sense to go to fancy restaurants alone at a time when you're likely to be most well received. Monday and Tuesday nights can be especially good times to try the glitzier places. On Friday and Saturday nights, even regular customers may be clawing each other for tables. So, if you go on either of those evenings, it isn't really surprising that a maître d' may try to stick you behind a potted palm. I try, when by myself, to seek out cheery restaurants just this side of funky. Rarely have I felt ill at ease, for instance, in a Chinese or Japanese restaurant, where the atmosphere tends to be more down-home than in the places the Michelin inspectors just left. I also make a point of trying fancier restaurants for breakfast or lunch, instead of for dinner, and not just because it's cheaper. You're more likely to be surrounded by loving couples in the evening, so a meal during the daytime can make you feel a little less alone.

Many people urge single men and women to tote newspapers or a hefty book to read while eating out. Those are fine for coffee shops and smaller places but will rarely do in restaurants that sport white table linens and Limoges china. I like to carry a small notebook in which to tally my expense account or record my impressions of my fellow diners. The notebook also lets me jot down ideas for a speech or interview the next day or to go over notes I've taken on a meeting with someone else. In a restaurant that does a heavy expense-account business, it seems very natural to see people going over notes, and no one needs feel conspicuous about it.

Yet it's increasingly less necessary for single people to feel conspicuous regardless of where they eat out. Go alone to a fancy restaurant—and you may feel far less isolated than you think. Lots of business travelers go to them alone, even though they are married. And, as in so many other areas of life, great adventures can result when you venture into uncharted terrain. Noticing that you are alone, people will approach you. Waiters will strike up conversations, and people at other tables may send you a drink. Sometimes you can even catch the eye of another solitary diner—something you couldn't do if you simply stayed in and ate Stouffer's—and by the time you leave the restaurant not feel alone at all.

8

Minding Your Money
(*What* Money?)

> "Nothing buys happiness, but money can cer-
> tainly rent it for short periods in expensive restau-
> rants or careless weeks on Austrian skis."
>> Irma Kurtz, as quoted by Liz Smith, in
>> the New York *Daily News*, April 13, 1978

Not long ago, a single adult's biggest financial decision was
whether to live uptown or down, or which brand of ski poles
to buy for a vacation in Stowe. As an unattached adult, you
were supposed to be out living it up, not worrying yourself
about things like investments or even a budget—and, if
there was no money left over at the end of the week, so
what? Your single years weren't going to last forever, and
your wedding day was soon enough to start being as sober
and responsible about money as were your parents, who
somehow never got over the Depression.

In recent years, much of this has changed, and not just
because the economy has caused everybody to think harder
about money. The longer people stay single, or the more

often they get divorced, the more likely they are to discover that the appeal of poverty decreases with every year they remain unwed.

Voluntary poverty is one thing. If you have decided to return to graduate school for a Ph.D. in classics, who cares if you have to live for a few years on jug wine and scrambled eggs? Poverty has always been easier on the nervous system, not to mention on the wallet, when everybody around you is scrimping too. Someday you will look back on your economies and they will all seem worth it. Meanwhile, you can console yourself by going around quoting Cato and telling yourself about all the intangible riches you encounter daily, in a Greek Revival library with a Latin inscription above the columns.

People in the creative professions, too, may spend many of their single years trying to put one foot over the poverty line yet still believing their sacrifices are well worth it. Until his early thirties, actor Dustin Hoffman had never earned more than $3000 a year. "If my parents hadn't sent me money every week, I would never have survived," he told one reporter. Then Hoffman earned $17,000 for appearing in *The Graduate*, a movie that made him famous overnight. A month after the film opened, however, he was again without work—and lining up to collect $55-a-week unemployment checks.

But the calculated poverty of a graduate student or unpublished novelist is vastly different from the involuntary insolvency of someone who just hasn't figured out how to make his or her income cover expenses, even though everyone else seems to be doing it quite nicely. And the latter is more deadly, because it can afflict you at forty as easily as at twenty. There is no peace for the compulsive spender in any tax bracket because, the more he or she earns or has, the more he or she spends. I have known subeditors at publishing houses who financed round-the-world trips on $15,000-a-year salaries by brown-bagging peanut butter and jelly lunches and living in unfashionable New Jersey suburbs while everybody else was reserving tables at the Italian Pavilion and signing leases on Central Park West. I have also known Wall Street lawyers, making $75,000 a year, who were forever overdrawing their checking accounts and ducking the collection agents from American Express. Money, like beauty or happiness, is relative. How much you have depends, to a certain extent, on how much you think you need.

In these expensive times, everybody needs to be more careful with money than in the good old days, when $100 a month was what you spent on rent, not on dinner for two at a nice restaurant or a pair of tickets for the new Neil Simon play at the Shubert. But single people need to be especially careful. A married couple always has a built-in system of checks and balances; a joint checking account insures that one person can never spend too much without having to account for it to somebody. A single man or woman is his or her own credit bureau and can spend till fiscal Armageddon without having to explain a cash drain to anyone.

Something else, too, makes the financial situation of single people different from that of many couples. Two married people living in suburbia may well try to keep up with the Joneses. But the Joneses tend to represent a single standard, whether symbolized by the size of their swimming pool or the country club to which they belong. Single people often try to keep up not with one set of friends but with many, a practice that wreaks havoc with their spending habits. Ironically, however, the people they are trying to impress may turn out instead to be driven away by the thought of a lifetime wedded to someone who may one day pull up to the poorhouse in a late-model BMW.

Single men and women are also vulnerable to spending to relieve loneliness. The mere prospect of another long weekend without a date is enough to make many unattached men and women reach for their Visa cards and plane tickets to the Bahamas. I, too, know the feeling. One summer evening when it seemed as though the entire adult population of Manhattan had been evacuated to Fire Island in a civil-defense test run for a nuclear attack, I walked twenty-seven blocks to the Dover Deli on East Fifty-seventh Street, the only place in town that I was sure carried the then new $3.50-a-pound Famous Amos chocolate chip cookies. Then I proceeded to eat them, one by one, on my way home, straight out of the bag. By the time I got to my third-floor walk-up at Thirtieth and Lex, the cookies were nearly gone —a silent witness not just to my momentary extravagance but to my loneliness.

A little such spending isn't necessarily harmful. Couples may recharge their marital batteries with high-priced weekends at country inns or on palm-fringed islands. So why shouldn't single people, too, claim their relief? There are, in fact, a lot of unattached men and women whose major problem is that they do not allow themselves enough such indulgences and who therefore miss out on some of the unique joys of singlehood.

You enter the danger zone mostly when you are always spending to relieve loneliness—or when money provides the only means you have of holding emotional isolation at bay. Then you will never catch up, because what you are seeking can't be bought with a traveler's check. And the price of the search is steep because, without a little money in the bank, you are never really free. You can't take the course that might help you land a new job, move to the bigger apartment that might broaden your outlook on life as on your living room. And you certainly can't help a younger sister or cousin through college—and thereby gain a real sense of making a contribution to other people's children that you can't make to your own.

Most of all, without a little money in the bank and the knowledge that you can keep acquiring it, you will always be trying to get out of being single, because marriage represents your only hope of achieving a financially secure future. It used to be mostly women who looked to marriage for economic redemption, but so today do many men, who find themselves divorce-poor and unable to maintain their lifestyle without becoming part of another two-income couple.

Like dieters who insist, "But I don't eat that much," many single people genuinely believe they are trying to keep their spending within bounds. They pride themselves on having discovered a wonderful little Burmese restaurant where meals can be had for under five dollars not counting the wine and tip, neglecting to consider that they eat there five times a week. Or they delight in finding an $800 Calvin Klein evening gown knocked down to half price—a steal, even though they will wear it only as often as the congressional elections roll around. A single person's lot, they tell themselves, is not an easy one, and such indulgences make it easier to bear.

Off the Spending-Go-Round

The only way to stop overspending is to begin thinking now about how much you want to have in the bank in one year or five or ten, whether you marry or don't. A friend who's an accountant or tax lawyer—or just a better money manager than you are—might be willing to sit down with you to help you figure out how much you'd need to save to accumulate the sort of nest egg you want within a few years. So might one of the older friends or couples whom every single person needs to have in his or her life. The best bet of all for many single people is to sit down with a certified financial planner or someone who can help you evaluate all your economic needs: for insurance, for investments, for buying a house, and even for retirement planning. I'd opt for a financial planner who doesn't sell insurance or another service along with advice, known as a "fee-only" planner. That sort of expert may charge more than someone else but will never try to make up the difference by talking you into buying, for instance, a bigger disability policy than you really need. Check your Yellow Pages for "Financial Planning

Consultants" or write to the International Association for Financial Planning (5775 Peachtree, Dunwoody Road, Suite 120C, Atlanta, Georgia 30342), which can send you a list of the fee-only planners in your Zip Code area.

Even people who are convinced they can't save any more money than they are now—and that may mean nothing— can begin to reckon with their financial future simply by getting a better feel for what they are spending. Just as dieters often find they are finally able to lose weight once they stop trying to diet and just keep a record of what they are eating each day, so can a lot of free spenders begin to come to terms with their cash drain just by toting up where it is all going. You might think of this practice as simply auditing yourself. Begin by keeping a record of every cent you spend, for a couple of months, in a small notebook. Don't forget to include such low-visibility costs as the interest payment on your monthly credit-card statement. Then add up all of your totals in categories such as food, rent, and transportation. One financial planner has noted that the shock value of seeing these numbers for the first time may, in itself, be enough to motivate you a little harder to cut back.

Once you have some sense of where your money is going, you'll find it easier to pull in the reins as needed. It is also a good idea to put yourself on occasional financial diets. Have one week a month when you enjoy only free entertainment and see how many different sorts of it you can discover: lectures at local colleges, fashion shows at department stores, organ recitals at churches, nature walks in a state park, concerts under the stars. Or buy a pocket calculator with a memory and tally your expenses throughout the day. Try to see how little you can spend in a single twenty-four-hour period over the course of a month. Try to go for an entire month without incurring a single parking ticket or directory-assistance charge on your phone bill.

By concentrating on one task or category at a time, you are more likely to be successful than if you try to reduce expenses across the board, which can seem hopeless. You might find the job easier if you pick up one of the sample budget and net-worth evaluation work sheets available from many banks and brokerage houses. Free budget work sheets are also available from the National Foundation for Consumer Credit, Inc. (Suite 601, 8701 Georgia Avenue, Silver Spring, Maryland 20910).

Your Freedom Fund

With some sense of how much money you have coming in and going out, you will be that much better prepared to set up the financial security blanket that every single man or woman needs—an account that I call your freedom fund. This fund usually takes the form of an interest-bearing checking account or money market fund containing however much cash you need to buy you peace of mind in fat times as in lean. It aims less to protect you when disaster strikes than to free you to be your best self day in and day out. It isn't, in other words, the cash that will allow you to pay the rent if you get fired; it is the money that allows you to quit your job before you do or to take the marketing courses that will put you in line for the next promotion into the Public Relations Department at your company.

Although it makes the most sense to keep your freedom fund in whatever sort of account will pay you the highest interest rate, such as a money market fund or bank account pegged to money market rates, a case can also be made for keeping a small amount of money in a traditional savings account. If you are the sort of person who bounces checks even occasionally, a savings account insures that you will always have a clear unblighted bank reference to give prospective landlords and others who may be considering extending you credit. A savings account can also provide you with a way to obtain a low-interest "secured" loan when you need it. (A secured loan allows you to borrow money, up to the amount in your savings account, by turning over your passbook, which is kept by the bank until your loan is repaid.) Finally, if you're planning to buy a house someday and worry that you may find it hard to do so without a second income, remember that, when mortgage money is tight, most banks and savings and loans lend it first to their regular depositors. A long-standing savings account and a cordial relationship with a sympathetic banker may give you the extra edge you need to obtain a mortgage on the strength of a single signature alone.

IRAs in the Fire

Many young, single men and women find it tough to think of retiring from anything more distant than an exercise salon about to be condemned by the Fire Department. No matter how young you are, however, it makes sense to set up an individual retirement account (if you are employed by a company) or a Keogh Plan (if you are self-employed). Although you can't withdraw money from an IRA or Keogh Plan without incurring penalties until you are fifty-nine and a half, money sunk into an individual retirement account accumulates tax-free over the years. The result is that it compounds at an incredible rate; you can often make more money parking your savings in an IRA or Keogh Plan, even *if* you incur penalties for someday withdrawing some of it early.

Let's look at some numbers. Anybody who has a job, with or without income from self-employment, can sock away up to $2000 a year, tax free, in an individual retirement fund. This, of course, first reduces the amount of federal income tax you pay. (If your income is $30,000, you pay taxes on just $28,000.) Beyond that, the money in your account will compound much faster than in another sort of account, undepleted as it is by a tax bite. If you are a single, thirty-year-old man or woman who plunks a mere $2000 a year into an IRA paying ten percent per year, you would have $596,253 at retirement; in an IRA paying twelve percent, you would have $966,926 at sixty-five. Moreover, a self-employed person can open both an IRA and a Keogh Plan. Ask the accountant who does your taxes to give you further guidelines on how much you ought to be putting into what kind of account.

Finally, remember that setting up an individual retirement plan has intangible benefits, quite apart from making you feel like a future tycoon. Like voting in school board elections, having an IRA or Keogh Plan makes you feel like a certified grown-up instead of somebody who is always planning to become one. Even if nobody else knows how much or little you have in your account, it makes you feel better about yourself for knowing you have looked your future in the eye. I opened my own Keogh Plan, during a particularly lean year, with a deposit of a mere $350, less than I'd have earned for a single day's work during a good year. The act nonetheless made me feel as though I'd attained instant adulthood. I found myself looking for any excuse to mention my Keogh Plan in conversations, in much the same way that people who have just gotten married leap at every opportunity to say "my husband" or "my wife," always feeling good when I did. My individual retirement account has since then turned out to be at least as sound an investment as my monogrammed bath towels, but one that will never grow threadbare with age.

The truth is that nobody wants to reach sixty-five only to come to agree with Oscar Wilde: "When I was young, I thought money was the most important thing in life—and, now that I am old, I know it is." And the only way to insure that money will become less important to you as you get older, not more, isn't so much to work hard for your money but to make your money work hard for you.

That means, of course, that you'll eventually need to move beyond saving your money or even sinking it in an IRA and toward some more aggressive investments. So let's look, next, at what some of them might be.

Investments for Innocents

Leafing through the pages of publications devoted to personal investing, many people feel overwhelmed. These days, there are far too many places to put your money for anybody to be fully knowledgeable about all of them. You can go a little crazy even trying to keep up with them.

Yet neither can most people, except for the very rich, turn all of their investment decisions over to somebody else. For one thing, it's too expensive. For another thing, it's too nerve-racking not to know anything about what is really happening to your hard-earned cash. Even to get the most from the services of financial advisers, you need to understand a little about the investments they might suggest for you.

All of this helps to explain why it's a good idea to begin any investment program by getting a little smarter about your range of options. A lot of adult or continuing education programs offer courses in money management for single people or in specialized investments such as limited partnerships in real estate. If such courses exist in your area and you believe you might benefit from them, by all means check them out.

Whether or not you take any classes, you'll still need to do some reading about the range of investments open to you. For starters, pick up a copy of *The Only Investment Guide You'll Ever Need* (Bantam, 1983), by Andrew Tobias. This handy paperback doesn't just live up to its title but is that rare financial guide that manages to give serious advice without sounding stuffy. Tobias has also put together a software program called "Managing Your Money" that, even at $200, has become a best-seller.

Another good idea is to take out a subscription to *Money* magazine (Rockefeller Center, New York, New York 10020), possibly the single most reliable source of advice for the neophyte investor. Though books and software programs can provide useful background material, only a magazine or newspaper can provide continually updated information that reflects fast-breaking market conditions and rates of return on many investments. The editors at *Money*, in recent years, have shown a refreshing and perhaps unique sensitivity to the financial concerns of single people, including the newly divorced or widowed, who are often featured in its "One Family's Finances" series or elsewhere in the magazine. As a sometime contributor to that magazine, I have also found that few publications pay closer attention to the accuracy of their facts.

Most people who read up on possible investments soon begin to think seriously about picking one or more of them to put some money into—and especially to consider playing the stock market. Before you do, it's a good idea to play the market on paper for three to six months. Pick out a half dozen or so companies that interest you: maybe because you've heard good things about them from family members who've worked or done business with them, because they manufacture products you use and like, or because they are headquartered in your area and you always seem to be reading about them in the local paper. Then chart the progress of their stocks on paper over the time period you have selected. This will give you more than a feel for how the stocks that might interest you are performing. It will also give you a better—and crucial—sense of how the stock market as a whole works. And one of the things you are likely to learn from your paper investing is simply this: that *when* you buy stock is as important as *what* you buy, because all stocks tend to be affected by the same broad economic forces affecting society as a whole. Often as not, when one of your stocks goes up or down, your others will tend to do the same thing. So it's more important to keep your eye on broad economic trends than it is to pounce on that rare hot tip from your brother-in-law or from last Friday night's date.

When you feel ready to begin playing the market for

keeps, you'll usually need a stockbroker. Some are happy only to place buy-and-sell orders that you give them; others like to pick and choose stocks for you after you've outlined your broad financial goals. So try to talk to several stockbrokers before you choose the one with whom you'll work. Ask your friends for recommendations or just stop into the office of any well-known firm and ask the manager to refer you to someone you can talk to about your needs.

One way to bypass the broker's office is to buy stocks by mail through the Merrill Lynch Sharebuilder Plan (P.O. Box 520, Church Street Station, New York, New York 10008). This plan allows you to buy individual stocks or fractions thereof for as little as $25 per transaction. Instead of calling your personal stockbroker, you send your order in to Merrill Lynch, where one of its representatives places your order for you and sends you a written record of the transaction. Members of the Sharebuilder Plan receive quarterly financial statements and an 800 number to call when questions rise.

Another way to invest without seeing a stockbroker is to buy shares in one or more of the mutual funds that are available directly from their seller, either by mail or in person. This can make sense for reasons besides convenience, especially if you're a beginner. One is that a mutual fund is a diversified group of stocks or other investments selected by professional money managers, so buying shares in one spreads your financial risk out instead of placing it all on one stock or bond. Another advantage to investing in a mutual fund is that you can keep track of its progress no less easily than that of a stock, because daily mutual fund prices are published along with the stock tables in most papers. Many funds, finally, are intended to be held for months or even years, which means you can often use one essentially as a savings account with a better rate of return. In fact, just as the financial experts of a generation ago urged people to put a little money in a savings account each week, no matter what, so do many of today's advisers encourage them to put a little money in a mutual fund each week or month, regardless of how the stock market as a whole is doing.

One way to learn more about the different kinds of funds available to you is simply to keep up your subscription to *Money*, which publishes regular reports on them. It also runs a monthly column called "Fund Watch" that lists the current yields of the top-ranked ones. *Forbes* magazine ranks the mutual funds annually in its last issue in August, a good one to pick up and hold onto throughout the year.

The best way to learn more about a particular fund that interests you is simply to write to the company that manages it for a prospectus and, if it is available by mail, an application form. One that has grown especially popular in recent years is the Fidelity Magellan Fund (82 Devonshire Street, Boston, Massachusetts 02109), selected as the top-performing mutual fund between 1978 and 1983 by Lipper Analytical Services. During those years, it gained 462 percent for shareholders who reinvested all their dividends. Other funds that have produced consistently high yields over a number of years include these, each of which is followed by its average annual yield between 1970 and 1982: The Janus Fund (100 Filmore Street, Suite 300, Denver, Colorado 80206), 18.4 percent; the Twentieth Century Growth Fund (P. O. Box 200, Kansas City, Missouri 64141), 21.5 percent; the International Investors Fund (122 East Forty-second Street, New York, New York 10168), 18.6 percent; and the Pioneer II Fund (60 State Street, Boston, Massachusetts 02109), 18.5 percent. Before you buy shares in these or any other funds, always write for a prospectus and the most recent performance figures.

Then there exist other mutual funds that aim not just to fatten your bank account but to soothe your social conscience. These specialize in what are sometimes called ethical investments, because their managers seek out companies that actively promote the common good—or at least do a minimum of harm. One of the better known is the Calvert Social Investment Fund (1700 Pennsylvania Avenue N.W.,

Washington, D.C. 20000). Its managers avoid investing in the nuclear and defense industries and in companies with substantial holdings in South Africa. Instead they tend to favor such companies as the American Indian Bank and People Express, the low-cost airline in which all employees are stockholders. At this writing, the advisory council for the Calvert Social Investment Fund includes such people as Julian Bond, the civil rights activist, and Robert Rodale, chairman of the Rodale Press, publisher of books on organic gardening and farming. Other mutual funds specializing in ethical investments might avoid buying stock in companies that get all or most of their earnings from the sale of alcohol, tobacco, or drugs. Or they might seek out those that aim to protect the environment, promote equal opportunity, or raise the level of consumer-product safety. The way to find a fund that matches your special interest is simply to write to several and inquire about their current holdings. Among those you might want to investigate are: the Pax World Fund (224 State Street, Portsmouth, New Hampshire 03801); the Foursquare Fund (24 Federal Street, Boston, Massachusetts 02110); and the Dreyfus Third Century Fund (c/o Bank of New York, Dreyfus Mutual Funds, P.O. Box 12135, Newark, New Jersey 07101).

Naturally, mutual funds aren't the only good investments for single people. Depending on the state of the economy as a whole, you might want to keep all or part of your money in a money market fund, in certificates of deposit, or in U. S. Treasury bills. And what about bonds, especially the tax-free ones issued by cities and states? Though these can also make good investments, they often require a minimum investment of $5000 or more, and they tie your money up for a fixed period, often many years. And, when you've got a chunk of cash that you won't need to touch for years, your best bet is almost always a house or condo or co-op.

The Case for Owning a Home

Not many people need to be reminded of the long-term financial benefits of owning a home. Neither do most single men or women need to be told how wonderful it would be not to have to go on bended knee to a landlord or building superintendent every time the baseboards need to be painted.

For most single people, though, home ownership has benefits that go far beyond either of those advantages. One is that almost nothing else can do so much to make you think of yourself as a full-fledged adult—a feeling some people get from marriage. Another benefit is that home ownership draws you deeper into the life of a community. A deed of your own gives you an added reason to be concerned about things such as zoning board meetings and an upcoming property tax referendum. Once you own a house, co-op, or condo, you tend to live *with* a neighborhood instead of just *in* it. You have roots, something single people, especially those over thirty, sorely need.

The bad news is that real estate prices have gone through the roof and show no signs of retreating. The ironic result is that—now that it has become socially acceptable and laws have made it possible for single people to own homes as readily as married ones—it often takes two incomes just to be able to meet a mortgage payment.

Yet single people hoping to buy homes usually have at least one advantage that married ones don't: they are rarely forced into making a too hasty purchase necessitated by the untimely arrival of a child or by the transfer of one member of a couple. Somebody who is single usually has the luxury of looking for a long, long time for something that is both affordable and appealing. During your years on your own, you can spend your summers driving up and down the coast until you find a tiny, nineteenth-century cottage, with gray cedar shingles and porthole windows overlooking the ocean, surrounded by drifts of blue hydrangeas and a tangle of wild rose vines. You can spend your nights fixing up a tumbledown baby Victorian or your weekends working with an architect to design a solar-heated retreat that lets you watch deer nibble on birch leaves through a plate-glass window or go cross-country skiing out your back door.

A married couple may have to make sacrifices, trading architectural dash for proximity to a decent school system or a big backyard for proximity to both spouses' offices. A single person can keep looking until finding a place that appeals to the heart as to the bankbook. Never again may you have the chance to live in a home that looks as though it had been built for you alone, partly because it was bought by you alone and you fixed it up entirely according to your own tastes.

When to Buy

Be careful, however, of buying when you plan to live in a community for only a year or two. Most real estate agents agree that, although spectacular profits can sometimes be made in a shorter time, you generally need at least three years of home ownership to be sure of being able to recoup the money you sank into buying and insuring your place, including what you've spent for nonrecoverable costs such as those for title searches. Neither does it make sense to buy a house if you're considering a major career change that could slash your income, or simply if owning a home would force you to give up too many things that seem to make life worth living, such as vacations or occasional trips to the opera. The purpose of buying a place is to increase the enjoyment you get from life—not to wipe it out.

Otherwise, though, you almost can't buy too soon. The law of what goes up must come down may not apply to mortgage rates. Even the fixed-rate mortgage itself appears to be an endangered species, as banks increasingly require variable-rate mortgages renewable and subject to change every few years.

One excellent way to begin to get a feel for what you might be able to afford in your area is to watch the real estate columns of your local paper for listings, under "Houses for Sale," of open houses at currently available properties. These allow you to bypass the realtor's office by simply showing up at a house or condo at a designated hour, when an owner or realtor will be on hand to explain the terms of the sale while giving you a tour. Though some will turn away people whom they don't perceive to be serious lookers, you may be able to prevent that from happening by dressing as though you mean business, or by taking a friend of the other sex with you (since, alas, couples may still be perceived as more serious buyers than single people).

Another idea is to try to sit down at your leisure, well before apartment living begins to chafe, and to figure out how much you might realistically be able to pay for a home. Include how much you'd need to be able to come up with for a down payment, as well as for monthly mortgage bills, utilities, and property taxes. Seek the aid of a friend who's a lawyer, an accountant, or a realtor, if you need to, in order to get some accurate figures. I've just purchased a dandy book of mortgage tables, at a stationery store, listing the amounts you'd have to pay for houses of varying costs at different interest rates. One such volume lists the payments you'd have to make on mortgages up to $100,000, at interest rates from ten to twenty percent. Entitled the Financial Comprehensive Mortgage Payment Tables (Publication 592 Revised), it is published by the Financial Publishing Company, 82 Brookline Avenue, Boston, Massachusetts 02115. If you can't find a similar one in your area, see if a stationer or bookseller will order it for you. Many banks or savings and loan associations provide similar tables free to prospective customers.

Getting some realistic numbers is essential because, with most homes these days going for something in the six-figure range, it is easy to misjudge what you can or can't afford. Let's say, for instance, that you've got your eye on a modest $60,000 house or condo. Let's also assume that you've been able to scrape together $10,000 for a down payment and will therefore need a $50,000 mortgage. According to the handy book of mortgage tables mentioned earlier, a $50,000 twenty-five-year mortgage, at fifteen percent would require monthly payments of about $640, or roughly the cost of a studio or one-bedroom apartment in many large cities. That figure, of course, doesn't count what you'd have to pay for property taxes and such. But neither does it take into account the tax deductions you'd be able to claim for the interest payments on your mortgage and the property tax, among other things. So the cost of owning a home, in the long run, may turn out to be more manageable than you think. That's all the more likely to be true if you rent a portion of your property to someone else, which would allow you to qualify for other tax breaks.

How to Beat the No-Down-Payment Blues

As most single people eventually discover, the monthly carrying costs of owning a home might not turn out to be more than what they'd pay for an apartment. It's coming up with the down payment that's the killer, more so today than ever. Whenever the housing market tightens, banks begin to require larger down payments than when more money was available—and today these can be as high as twenty percent for a house and a staggering forty percent for a condo. It's almost enough to make you give up on looking for a place even before you start.

But there are ways to beat the no-down-payment blues. One is simply to consider borrowing what you need from a parent or another close relative. Back when your mother and father bought their first home, it was almost a given that people would obtain help from their parents, and it is increasingly necessary for the current generation of single people to do the same. If you want to retain your financial and emotional independence, have a lawyer draw up a document that specifies the terms under which you'll pay your family members back or cut them into a share of the profits. If it isn't pulling together the down payment but getting a mortgage that's your problem, see if your parents or another relative will cosign one for you.

It's also not a bad idea to consider buying a home with a friend, particularly if you live in an area that has a lot of two- or even three-family homes that would allow each buyer to have his or her own floor. In my city, such double- and triple-deckers abound, often testifying to their multiple ownership by stories painted different colors, such as blue and brown, in a whimsical architectural parfait. The six-figure home, off limits to many single people, becomes far easier to afford when more than one buyer is involved. Three single women I know recently purchased a triple-decker home, for slightly over $100,000, in a section of Cambridge, Massachusetts, so fashionably tweedy that it would sink if leather elbow patches were heavier. Each woman paid a down payment of about $5,000, and after that, monthly carrying costs based on her $33,000 portion of the mortgage. Each woman's investment bought her an entire floor of a house with a huge porch and backyard in a neighborhood none of them could have afforded to buy into on her own.

Joint home purchases can make sense even when you could afford to buy on your own. They may simply leave you more leeway to take Caribbean vacations or give you someone with whom to share the burden of fixing up a run-down place. A friend may have a better head than you do for fuse boxes or plumbing and thus spare you some of the mistakes you might make on your own.

And there increasingly exist other options for the cash-poor home buyer. Somebody who's especially eager to un-load a particular piece of property might be willing to make special concessions to induce you to buy. He or she might agree to forgo a down payment in return for receiving bigger monthly checks, or might put off receiving the down payment for a couple of years, until you've had more time to get your finances together. Watch newspapers for sales featuring "seller financing" or "assumable mortgages," either of which may offer you the sort of deal you need.

Another relatively recent innovation is the "shared equity" concept, which enables cash-poor home buyers to join forces with cash-rich investors. Under shared equity plans, the buyers of a home agree to put up all monthly carrying costs. The investors put up the down payment in return for a piece of the profits when the property is later sold or refinanced. A free brochure explaining the procedure can be obtained by sending a stamped, self-addressed legal-sized envelope to: C. Peterson, the Ticket Corporation, 233 Brookcliff Trace, Marietta, Georgia 30067, which has operated such programs in more than twenty states.

Up from Condomania

When you're finally ready to buy, which makes more sense: a condo, a co-op, or a home? Sometimes the answer is obvious: a condo or co-op may be the only thing you can afford to buy in the neighborhood you want to live in. This tends especially to be true when you have your heart set on putting down roots in the most fashionable section of a large city, such as Philadelphia's Society Hill or Washington, D.C.'s Georgetown. The nineteenth-century brick row houses on my own Beacon Hill start at about $250,000 and go up in price to three or four million, making them off limits to the overwhelming majority of single people. A condo can be had for about $50,000 per room, with a one-bedroom unit including kitchen and bath generally costing $100,000 to $150,000. Though the price tag is steep, it might seem worth it if you yearn for gas lights, brick sidewalks, and window boxes abloom with geraniums in the spring.

Another advantage to buying a co-op or condo is that it gives you an instant community of people with whom you have at least one important, shared interest. And their presence can help to alleviate many worries about owning a home for the first time. You won't be the only one who has to make a fast decision on what to do when the oil burner breaks down for the eleventh time on a cold January morning. All such decisions will be made jointly by you and the others in your condominium trust or co-op association, and by participating in the process you can learn a lot that may aid you when you need to make similar choices without help.

But condos and co-ops are far from a fail-safe investment. It isn't just that many lending institutions require you to put up that whopping forty percent down payment mentioned earlier, on the theory that the relative newness of such investments makes them riskier than others. All future buyers of your unit may have to put up a similarly high amount, making it harder for you to resell it.

Condos and co-ops also have proved to be more volatile investments than single-family homes. In some cities, entire buildings filled with them sit empty, because the economy of the country as a whole changed between the time a developer drew up plans and when the construction was finally completed. The last time I looked for a rental apartment, I was shown many condos that had been placed on the market by owners who had despaired of trying to sell their properties—and were now simply looking for a way to be able to pay their property taxes and meet their monthly carrying costs. Like hot growth stocks, condos and co-ops have also been oversold in many areas by the media, with the result that they may carry vastly inflated price tags.

It also goes without saying that their management can be fraught with peril. Not all condo or co-op associations govern their buildings harmoniously. In some, bitter disputes have erupted over such small matters as the cost of fixing cracks in the front sidewalk, with the result that next-door neighbors wound up barely speaking to each other.

Finally, unlike single-family homes, condos and co-ops generally become places you want to move out of. So they give you less of the feeling of permanence for which many single people come to long. They are also far less likely to come with the patch of adjoining land, in the form of a terrace or porch, that can make you feel as though you are really living.

Still, there's no question but that, when condo or co-op ownership works, it can do so beautifully. One divorced man dreaded weekends in his rambling Dutch colonial home in the suburbs—a feeling he nonetheless endured so that his two children would have grass underfoot when they came to visit. Then he discovered a townhouse condominium complex a mere two miles down the road. It came complete with tennis courts, a swimming pool, and a community room where birthday and other parties were held for the owners and their offspring. The complex turned out to provide an ideal compromise between city and suburban living. The father got a place to live that made him feel less isolated than a house and that didn't require so much maintenance. The children got trees, grass, recreational facilities, and lots of others their own age to play with. Today, the same children look forward to the day when they will grow up and own, not a dream home, but a condo "just like Daddy's."

9

Club Med and Beyond, or The Delights of Traveling Alone

Travel ought to be one of the great pleasures of being single. After all, when will you again have so many opportunities to light out on your own for Athens, Acapulco, or even Atlantic City? At least one great destination a year should beckon so irresistibly that you can't pass it up.

The reality is, however, that most single people don't travel nearly so often as they could or would like to. Let midsummer roll around, and you will likely find them visiting their families in Booniesville or stretched out with a book on a chaise longue beside the apartment-complex pool. Never mind that you can read the new James Clavell novel anytime, anywhere, but that the beaches of Nice are at their best in July. Like so many other things you can do when you are single, taking the trip of a lifetime tends to take a back seat to more accessible pleasures. And that is frankly a sad state of affairs, because any number of wonderful vacations are best taken without a partner—and some of them may never be possible again.

Ask any couple you know: marriage limits your mobility,

and children restrict it even more. The midwinter vacation in Cancun can give way to a landscaping job for the lawn or the annual European fling to private schools for the children. A lot of married couples used to board a 747 as easily as the IRT. Now they can scarcely find a baby-sitter to mind the store while they go to the movies, let alone find someone to watch two youngsters and a beagle while they hop off to Marrakesh. Life has changed—and they with it.

Quite apart from whether you'd be able to travel so often after marriage, you'd inevitably do so less freely. Once you have wed, a spouse's preferences must be considered. At best, vacations are a compromise: one year you go where you want, the next year where your partner wants, and sometimes you go where you have to—to the in-laws' instead of to the ski slopes or to a family reunion instead of Ibiza.

Then, too, society has not yet become so liberated that couples usually travel separately during their vacations. In even the most progressive marriages, a husband and wife tend to go away together or not at all, except on business. This may someday rule out destinations that simply don't appeal to a spouse as much as they do to you or those best enjoyed by yourself. Not many couples go together to health spas, to photography workshops, or even to tennis camps, all of which can provide wonderful vacations for single people.

Make no mistake, however: traveling when you are single is more than an insurance policy against future deprivations. It is also one of the best means you have to keep exposing yourself to the sort of new experiences that your children might draw you into . . . if you *had* children. Travel can thereby go a long way toward keeping you from feeling that your life is going stale and giving you something to look forward to from one year to the next.

Regular travel can also go a long way toward keeping you from feeling sorry for yourself for being single. Unmarried life admittedly can feel a bit small and crabbed at times, and married couples' existences can seem somehow jazzier. (Never mind, of course, that they sometimes look at yours with the same sort of envy.) By continually reaching out to new destinations, you keep enlarging your life and thereby insuring that your friends won't feel sorry for you either. A woman named Samantha swears that, the last time two of her smugly married acquaintances were going on about "poor little Sam" and how they hoped she'd find a husband soon, she looked at them levelly. "But I couldn't possibly get married," she insisted. "It would interfere with the trip I'm planning to Bora Bora." Thereupon she pulled out her snapshots of last year's barge trip down the Nile, leaving her married friends lamely chipping in with the details of a Saturday at Jungle Habitat. Who, after all, was to feel sorry for whom?

By "traveling" I do not mean only going on long voyages. I mean visiting any place you've never seen before, whether three miles from home or three thousand. If you live in a small town and have never gone anywhere but on a class trip to Valley Forge, traveling could mean lighting alone, for the first time, for a weekend in the big city. If you already live in a metropolis, it could mean touring an unfamiliar section of it on a sightseeing bus jammed with out-of-towners. One of my favorite mini-vacations is boarding a Gray Line bus, in the city I now live in, for a day trip to a historic suburb. As a New Yorker, I often took the Sunday afternoon walking tours of city neighborhoods, sponsored by the Museum of the City of New York. All were so rich in detail that I never came away from them without feeling that I had seen my city anew. Such trips have refreshed and recharged me no less than the longer ones. Yet single people have a unique opportunity to take more important trips to places they may never again have a chance to see. So let's look now at some easy ways to indulge your wanderlust, beginning with a popular form of travel too often overlooked by single men and women.

Just Cruising

A cruise can offer a wonderful way to unwind, explore new ports of call, and savor many of the amenities of a posh resort, without being cooped up in the same spot for a week. Nonetheless, a lot of single people react to the idea of a shipboard vacation with about as much enthusiasm as they'd have for two weeks in an armored tank. The presumed disadvantages of a cruise are these:

1. On a ship you will never make friends with people of your own age, at least if you are under sixty, because most cruises look like floating Gray Panthers' conventions.

2. On a ship you will pay more than you would elsewhere, because anyone traveling without a partner will get slapped with a singles supplement that will send you directly into Chapter Eleven.

3. On a ship you will be bored bleary and reduced to doing nothing but playing shuffleboard and watching your waistline expand from all the Napoleons you consume at meals.

4. On a ship you will absolutely never have a prayer of finding romance, because the ratio of single women to men is approximately nineteen thousand to one, thereby insuring that any female traveler except Jessica Lange will be immediately clobbered by the competition, and any male traveler will be so overwhelmed by the pursuing hordes that he will have to barricade himself inside his stateroom just to finish his new Peter De Vries novel by the time the ship docks in Freeport.

Now let's look at some realities:

1. Some forty percent of all cruise passengers are under thirty-five. One long-established tour packager that offers many cruises exclusively for people under thirty-five is Singleworld (444 Madison Avenue, New York, New York 10022). And many steamship lines aren't just attracting a younger set but are offering activities for them, such as

singles parties, aerobic dance classes, and mini-courses in subjects like Chinese cooking or computer literacy.

2. Most cruise lines *do* require unmarried travelers to book double cabins, for which they may pay seventy-five percent more than they would with a per-person, double-occupancy rate. Some lines, however, have started to accommodate single travelers by setting up programs that guarantee to match you with roommates of the same sex or to give you a double room at a lower rate. One such company is Cunard, which has offered a room-sharing plan on its seven-day Caribbean cruises on the *Countess* and the *Princess*. At this writing, Singleworld offers a roommate-finding service for its trips to the Caribbean and Mexico, and most of its trips offer a social calendar with singles cocktail parties and other events.

The prices you pay for cruises are almost never as low as those you'd pay for, let's say, a rock-bottom charter flight. But you can wind up spending less in the long run, because most of your meals and entertainment are provided, thereby removing from your reach the temptation to overspend. Some cruises, finally, offer programs that let you travel for free or at a drastically reduced rate if you can round up a specified number of friends who'll go with you— a great idea for single people who work in offices with a lot of unattached men or women who can never figure out where to go over the holidays.

3. On a ship you won't necessarily enjoy the same activities you would if you spent a week on dry land, so in that sense boredom might seem more of a threat. But most cruises these days offer far more than playing shuffleboard, sipping cocktails in the Captain's Lounge, or trying to remember where you put your Dramamine. Many ships feature such diversions as movies, language classes, swimming pools, discos complete with dance lessons, seminars led by the sort of psychologists you can see on "Donahue," and mini-health spas for people who don't want to gain weight while they gain new experiences. Onshore excursions tend

to be equally varied. A Mexican cruise might give you a chance to poke around in the Mayan ruins at Chichén Itzá, a Virgin Islands fling let you try scuba diving in St. Thomas.

4. Although women still outnumber men on most cruises (which, of course, isn't necessarily a drawback if you are a single man), even that seems to be changing. Some tour packagers, such as Singleworld, try to have more balanced ratios when possible. In any case it's usually possible to learn the male-female mix on your particular trip before you set sail.

More important, however, is that romance is the last thing you ought to be looking for on vacation, nice as it is to find it when it turns up unexpectedly. Like taking courses or visiting museums, traveling is a pleasure in its own right that shouldn't be co-opted by being turned into a search for romance. It is something to do just for you, whether or not it ever turns up somebody else.

Besides, it's hard to think of a more depressing way to live than to believe that only your two-week annual vacation might turn up any romance that is lacking from your life. If you ache for more companionship from the other sex, the thing to do isn't to pin all your hopes on the chance that a single trip will turn it up; it's to beef up the rest of your life so that it includes more opportunities for connecting accidentally with prospective dates. Otherwise, you may ruin not just your vacation but a lot of the moments when you look back on it.

A few other advantages of a cruise, finally, ought not to be overlooked. One is that something about being out on the water makes you feel miles away from whatever is bothering you, be it a romance that's gone flat or the draconian politics at your office. The gentle lapping of waves against a boat or the hum of its engines can lend a soothing and almost primal quality to your experiences, and one you are unlikely to find in a train station in Marseilles or in the crush deplaning at Heathrow. (And even seasickness isn't so much of a problem as it used to be on ships, because their stabilizers are more effective.) What I call the "soothe factor" of a cruise makes it an especially good sort of vacation to take when you're feeling a bit trampled by life and in need of psychic restoration. Finally, cruises give many single people the all too rare pleasure of being served and even coddled, which can be a rare treat when you're used to meeting all your own needs.

If you aren't sure you'd like the feeling of being out on a big boat, watch newspapers for advertisements of the popular "Cruises to Nowhere" that some steamship lines have recently begun to offer. Often exclusively for single people, these "cruises" are really floating cocktail parties that allow you to spend a few hours or days circling a harbor on an ocean liner that's pulled into port between trips. This is a fun way to meet people that can also help you try the idea of boat travel on for size.

Cruises can also be among the easiest vacations to prepare for. Taking a trip to Europe or elsewhere often requires getting a passport, or shots, exchanging American dollars for foreign, and trying to converse with natives in your lame high school French. Taking a cruise often requires only proof of citizenship, such as a birth certificate. You just visit a travel agent or cruise line, then get on board and go.

Finally, cruises can be the best or only way to sample many destinations in a short time. There's really no cost-effective way to see a half dozen Caribbean islands in a week or so, for instance, except by taking a cruise. And, after giving a lot of alluring spots the once-over, you can more easily decide which ones you'd like to return to later on—not to mention which ones you'd never want to visit on the honeymoon you may yet have.

Good Things in Tour Packages

Ask most single people why they don't travel more often, and you are likely to hear that plaintive lament: "But I have nobody to travel *with.*"Never mind that most have friends, roommates, or relatives who might make excellent companions on a journey. The point of taking a vacation, it seems, is precisely to get away from all of the people who might accompany you on it.

Not everybody, however, enjoys traveling alone, and some destinations are frankly too remote or unsafe to be hazarded on your own. Besides, it's nice to have somebody with whom you can later share your memories of Perugia or Port-au-Prince.

Apart from taking a cruise, there are two effective ways to beat the nobody-to-travel-with blues. One is to go with a group of people who assemble at your point of origin—to take some sort of tour. The other is to travel alone to your destination and to connect with others after you get there. Neither approach is inherently preferable to the other, so let's look first at some of the tours you can take, if only because they are so often overlooked by single people who fear they will be filled with couples on their honeymoon or celebrating their fiftieth anniversary.

It's important to note, for starters, that there are both "escorted" and "packaged" tours. The former generally provide everything you need for an entire vacation, including your air fare, hotel rooms, airport transfers, sightseeing excursions, and a guide who accompanies you everywhere. Though many are too inflexible for most single people, others can be invaluable when you want to visit spots that you couldn't get to without the services of a guide or someone else to lead the way. A lot of overseas trips would simply be too hard to arrange on your own. Not many travelers, for instance, would want to be left on their own for even a day or two during an African safari, a boat trip on the Amazon, or a camping excursion in the Australian outback. To enjoy any of those trips expeditiously, you need to put yourself in the hands of an escorted-tour service, such as Questers Worldwide Nature Tours, 257 Park Avenue South, New York, New York 10010. On all trips, Questers allows single travelers to request a roommate. If the organization can't find one for you, it will give you a single room at no extra charge.

If you want to visit less exotic locations, you're usually better off with a flexible packaged tour. Many such trips provide only your plane ticket, hotel rooms, and perhaps a few extras. Especially popular among single people are the packaged tours run by International Weekends (IW) Charter Vacations, Inc. (National Reservations Center, 1170 Commonwealth Avenue, Boston, Massachusetts 02134), known as much for its lack of rigidity as for its low prices. Many IW tours include only air fare, lodging, airport transfers, and a welcoming get-together for guests, leaving participants free to plan their own days. Optional side trips may be available for those with a higher threshold for group activity. For an additional ninety-nine dollars above the cost of any trip, IW will find you a roommate, or provide you with a single room for that amount of money. Look for ads for IW trips in the Sunday New York *Times* and note the prices and departure dates of trips that might interest you. A week or two before a tour is scheduled to leave, prices may be slashed further, turning up especially good deals. You can find out more about these by calling or writing IW to ask about its "Best Buys" of the week.

You can often find out about other interesting tours by joining groups or institutions that meet a specialized need. Almost every large city, for instance, has a major museum whose curators lead art tours for members. Once you've paid a membership fee, often as low as twenty-five dollars, you'll be notified of upcoming trips, perhaps to important art galleries in Europe or elsewhere. Many museums also offer day trips to artists' studios close to home, a nice way to see another side of your city. If no museum in your area sponsors art tours abroad, consider joining the Friends of the Harvard Art Museums (32 Quincy Street, Cambridge, Massachusetts 02138), which helps to arrange travel programs led by the faculty of the country's most prestigious university.

Single people who are more interested in sports than in culture often enjoy the tours on foot or bike sponsored by the American Youth Hostels, Inc. (1332 I Street N.W., Suite 800, Washington, D.C. 20005). Don't let the word "youth" throw you; this venerable organization is open to all ages and does far more than help people find hostels, or low-cost places to stay, in the United States and Europe. It also sponsors foreign tours to points as distant as China and Japan. Trips are organized along age lines (so that, if you're a young, single adult, you needn't find yourself spending all your time in the company of golden agers). American Youth Hostels local councils sponsor other trips in the United States, including many day hikes. These take place even in big cities, including Manhattan, where members might stroll through Central Park or wend their way among skyscrapers. That makes AYH a great group to join even if this isn't your year to splurge on a European fling.

Similarly healthy and low-cost trips become available to men and women who join the Appalachian Mountain Club (5 Joy Street, Boston, Massachusetts 02114). In recent years, AMC members have hiked through Holland at tulip time and backpacked through the Norwegian fjords—not to mention taken countless trips in the United States. They have also taken any number of day or half-day hikes. And you needn't fear that, to enjoy them, you'd need the stamina of an Olympic athlete. All AMC hikes are geared to a particular level of ability—beginner, intermediate, or advanced—so almost anybody can enjoy them. As a longtime AMC member, I've gone on several of its trips and found them filled with single people.

Don't forget, finally, that almost every large association occasionally organizes trips for its members, often at prices far below what you'd pay if you booked your own tour. Among those that do are college alumni/ae organizations, men's and women's clubs, trade associations, and churches and synagogues. To find out about those trips, though, you've got to become a member, and, if you're already looking ahead to next summer, that means you may have to sign up now.

Summer (and Winter) Schools and Camps for Grown-ups

When you don't like to travel by yourself but don't want to take a cruise or a group tour, you can still enjoy your time off from work by going alone to a great destination—and then connecting with others after you get there. And that's especially likely to be true if you go to a summer school or camp for grown-ups that lets you learn while you enjoy your two weeks with pay.

Few educational vacations have attracted a wider following among single men and women than the wilderness survival schools run by Outward Bound (384 Field Point Road, Greenwich, Connecticut 06830). Although also open to married people, the Outward Bound programs have a special benefit for single ones: they provide such an intensely shared experience that participants may come to rely on each other no less than members of a family would, forming ties that last long after a vacation has ended. Those participants learn, among other things, to climb rocks, pitch tents, paddle kayaks and other boats, and forage for food among wild berries and plants. By doing so, they can also forge a vital tie to nature that is often missing from the lives of single people who spend much of their time cooped up in apartments.

The popular ecology camps run by the National Audubon Society (4150 Darley, Suite 5, Boulder, Colorado 80303) provide a gentler but no less educational experience. The society operates four camps—in Maine, Wisconsin, Connecticut, and Wyoming—with each one devoted to the exploration of a different sort of ecosystem. At all of the camps, single people share living quarters, three or four to a room, while married couples have private accommodations.

Ecology is also the focus of many trips put together by Earthwatch (10 Juniper Road, Box 127N, Belmont, Massachusetts 02178). This terrific organization matches researchers from universities around the world with lay volunteers who help with the scientists' experiments, often in remote locations. Earthwatch volunteers, ranging from teenagers to octogenarians, have helped scientists collect ice samples from a glacier in the Canadian Rockies and excavate archaeological sites in the Middle East. Most such trips are fourteen to eighteen days long. And, as a fabulous bonus, anything you pay to Earthwatch is tax-deductible.

Not, of course, that the great outdoors is the only thing you can contemplate during your time off from work. The following are some of the other means by which you can learn while you vacation:

• *Cooking Classes Abroad:* Anybody who's outgrown the cooking classes at the local adult ed center might want to take some lessons from a widely respected European chef. The problem is that most of the courses abroad are given in foreign languages. One place where many cooking classes are translated into English is at La Varenne (Ecole de Cuisine La Varenne, 34 Rue St. Dominique, 75007, Paris, France), the world-famous school at which many prominent American chefs have trained. The translations at La Varenne don't just insure that you'll understand what is really happening to the soubise sauce but that you'll be able to converse and perhaps see a few sights with your classmates after the instructions have been completed.

• *Computer Courses:* Almost everybody has read by now about the growing number of computer camps for kids. Less widely publicized has been the proliferation of similar camps for adults. At many you can swim or play tennis after you've had instruction and hands-on practice using one or more of the most popular models of home computers. One organization that runs such camps for adults is Computers Simplified (6515 Saroni Drive, Oakland, California 94611), which offers many programs for men and women with little or no experience with computers. Its classes usually take place in resort settings such as Palm Springs or Lake Tahoe over long, holiday weekends.

• *Writing and Photography Workshops:* A lot of single people find that keeping a journal makes life more interesting, but what can make keeping a journal more interesting? One answer is: going to a writers' workshop that lets you attend lectures by best-selling authors, many of whom keep diaries of their own. Only the most prestigious programs have competitive admissions policies; most are open to anyone who owns a battered Smith-Corona or an IBM PC. Look for a complete listing of them annually in the May issue of *The Writer* magazine (P. O. Box 892, Boston, Massachusetts 02117). Two popular photography workshops are the Maine Photographic Workshop (Rockport, Maine 04856) and the Travel Photography Workshop in Santa Fe (P. O. Box 2847, Santa Fe, New Mexico 87504). The latter consists of several one-week courses offered each September at the Hotel La Posada in New Mexico's capital city, so you might be able to fit in a workshop following another vacation spent somewhere else in July or August.

• *Tennis Camps:* Tennis is practically the national sport of single people, and there's no need to feel left out just because you didn't develop a backhand in childhood. Spend a week or two at a well-known tennis camp and you may do more for your game than you could in a week of Saturday mornings on the courts. Look for camp advertisements in the tennis magazines you see at your local newsstand or ask a travel agent about them. Remember, too, that there are camps for players of all levels, so even if you've never picked up a racquet you can still find one that will soon have you showing off your serve at a singles tennis party at a club near where you live.

- *Crafts Courses:* At the Haystack Mountain School of Crafts (Deer Isle, Maine 04627) adults can study weaving, ceramics, photography, graphic design, woodworking, or other crafts in an intensive two- or three-week instructional program. Haystack is probably what summer camp would have been like if you'd moved beyond making lanyards and weaving an occasional basket or two, to working on developing really polished skills. People who go there are generally serious learners; sports are almost nonexistent and on an island you don't easily run off to the mainland when the mood for diversion strikes. But at Haystack you may acquire skills that would take months to develop back home, not just because the instruction is more intensive than what you'd get from a private teacher or adult-ed class, but because you have many other serious students from whom to learn, too.

- *Camps with a Conscience:* Sometimes it can seem almost immoral to spend thousands or even hundreds of dollars on a sexy vacation in Europe or elsewhere, when so much of the world gets no vacation at all. One way to take your social conscience with you when you travel is to attend one of the annual series of seminars on such subjects as civil liberties, feminism, or global peace, sponsored by the World Fellowship Center (R.D. Box 136, Conway, New Hampshire 03818). Its programs take place every summer in the beautiful White Mountains and leave participants plenty of time for recreation. Paid babysitting can be arranged for single parents or others. More than forty years old, World Fellowship seeks "to bring together a diverse group of people from many different social, intellectual, and religious backgrounds," all at a low cost.

- *Club Med:* Finally, no word on summer or winter camps for adults would be complete without a mention of Club Med, which practically invented the concept. With dozens of resorts around the world, this organization has a vacation destination in almost any climate—and at almost any of them you will find single people.

Is Club Med right for you? That depends partly on your tolerance for communal activity, which has long been the name of the game at its resorts. Meals, sports, and parties are usually shared with others. Some clubs have offered private accommodations during the off season at a cost of thirty dollars extra per day. Usually, though, you'll have to share a room with a stranger unless you go with a friend or manage to connect with a kindred spirit on the plane.

Equally important is *which* resort you go to, because facilities tend to vary, not just in what they offer, but in their demographics. The Club Med on Martinique, for instance, has long had a reputation for attracting a young crowd, including many single people in their early twenties, which helps to give it a freewheeling ambience. The resort at Caravelle on nearby Guadeloupe tends to draw an older group, with more single men and women in their thirties, or even forties or fifties, and also a lot of married couples.

A few rules of common sense ought to prevail, in any case, when choosing a resort. If you don't want to wind up vacationing with a lot of children or college students, who flock to Club Med when classes are out, be careful about turning up during school vacations, such as during Christmas week. Remember, too, that part of the appeal of Club Med is that it is continually opening new resorts. So, if you like their flavor, you'll rarely lack for a fresh vacation destination. But it usually takes awhile for a new resort, run by Club Med or anyone else, to have all its kinks ironed out. And the glitches can be all the more annoying when you've booked yourself into a tropical island for a week and can't get away. So you might wait a season or two before checking out a new resort or at least try to talk with someone who's been there to get the early returns.

Another good idea is to visit the Club Med national reservations center at 3 East Fifty-fourth Street in Manhattan the next time you're in its neighborhood. There you can spend forty-five minutes or so viewing videotapes of its facilities around the world and spend as much time as you like getting your questions answered by its agents. If you can't pay that sort of visit, you can obtain information about resorts around the world by writing to the main office of the organization: Club Med, 40 West Fifty-seventh Street, New York, New York 10019.

Don't forget that today a lot of the same resorts offer special programs for children—great if you're a single parent, perhaps less so if you aren't. Some Club Med facilities also offer lessons and hands-on practice using Atari computers, which might be just the thing for somebody who can't bear to be too far away from modern technology, even on vacation.

10

Problems, Problems

A lot of what you read these days suggests that the worst problem any single person faces is the vertigo that results from spinning in a perpetual social whirl—or perhaps the eyestrain that might result from waking up to a different wallpaper pattern five mornings out of seven. To believe either, of course, is a little like believing that the worst problem a married couple faces is figuring out how to sing "Those Were the Days" in two-part harmony, while one spouse plunks out the tune on an old upright piano.

We will now observe a moment of silence for all stereotypes of married and single people—and good riddance to them. Lord knows, both groups have suffered from them long enough.

This is not necessarily to suggest that doing a solo run will never present problems. During your single years, you will unquestionably have moments when you feel you've been hit by a sixteen-wheeler on I-95 and left sprawled and bleeding on the shoulder, without so much as another adult for company. Such occasions are simply to be expected, just as it is to be expected that, if you were married, you would have moments when you'd glance longingly at your Hamilton Beach electric carving knife and wonder what it would be like to run it across your partner's throat.

Neither can you predict when the bad moments will hit. You can be cruising along on a freeway to success—happy with your work, your love life, and your friendships, among other things—when a roadblock suddenly arises to throw you completely off course. Or you can breeze by events that take a toll on other single people, such as the holidays or getting your pocket picked, but find yourself unexpectedly undone by the death of a pet or the wedding of a close friend.

Here, then, are some of the problems you may encounter in the single lane, plus some thoughts on how to approach each.

The Great Dinner Party Debacle

Most single people never experience such major problems as chronic loneliness or depression (though they, too, will be dealt with below). But almost all unattached men and women *do* face their quota of petty annoyances.

Take dinner parties, for instance. Or, to be more precise, take the people who give them. Not many hosts these days are so gauche as to ask a single man or woman not to come to a dinner party unless he or she can come with a date. A lot of hosts, however, achieve a similar effect in more subtle ways. They may invite you over only when they know they can invite someone *for* you. Or they may ask you to dinner only when they know you will want to come in tandem, such as when you are so deeply immersed in a romance that you couldn't be pried away from your love by a 260-pound nose guard for the Miami Dolphins. The hosts who insist on having you paired up often explain that they only want you to have a dinner partner "so you'll feel more comfortable." Few of them, though, would dream of excluding a black or a

Jew unless they could pair either of them up, too, let alone dream of insisting that they were only trying to insure the comfort of the black or the Jew.

Try nonetheless to be patient with the sort of overzealous hosts who always want to couple you up. They don't want you paired up for your comfort but for theirs. Then, too, their numbers grow smaller every year. So try to resist pointing out that you have mastered more difficult challenges than chewing your food without moral support from another unmarried adult.

If you care about hosts who insist on playing Noah, the best approach is to invite them to your place for dinner without inviting a date for yourself, an occasion that ought to demonstrate that your digestive tract doesn't require the presence of another single person to function. Better still, invite several couples at once, which will keep all of you so thoroughly occupied that no one may notice who has a partner and who doesn't.

Mercifully, some hosts do invite you over alone. They may even have the wit to realize that they need not invite someone for you. But they still tend to have you over mostly on occasions that seem earmarked for entertaining single people. Maybe you get asked to drop by for Chinese food after work while their married friends are wined and dined at sit-down Saturday night affairs. Or maybe you get invited to sprawling bashes attended by so many others that you would scarcely be noticed if you were a two-headed goat. You know you're grateful to be included, on whatever terms. But how nice it would be, you realize, if social events still weren't divided into categories for married and for single. Interestingly, the hosts who exclude single people don't do so because they feel their marriages are threatened by them. (In that case it might even be understandable—if you felt somebody else was after your partner, would you much enjoy spending an evening with that person?) Most people who exclude unpaired single men or women do so, rather, because they have always done things that way, and it doesn't occur to them to change. So use whatever occasions you can to do a little consciousness raising on the side, such as by explaining how much you appreciate it when you are invited over just for yourself.

The Black-Tie Blues

Like determinedly paired-up private parties, a lot of public events don't do any favors for the unattached, so the idea is just to get through them in whatever way feels most comfortable. Single people, for instance, are scarcely allowed in the door at any number of black-tie charity events. The unattached may also have to pay more per capita to attend than do married people, who often pay a discounted ticket price for couples. Then there exist all those tired company functions to which you are expected to bring a date, or risk getting passed over for promotion on the grounds that you are a self-declared social deviant.

Don't lose too much sleep over whom to bring to such pointedly paired-up public events. The important thing is just to be seen at them—and never mind with whom. Your best bet is often just to dredge up what is known in Washington, D.C., circles as a good "walker"—someone who escorts the wives of politicians to official functions when their husbands are away. This sort of person can be an old friend or distant relative. What matters is mostly that your walker have enough savvy not to drink from the finger bowls or ask for steak tartare rare. And, by all means, if you aren't stepping out with someone you're mad about, don't feel you have to blow an entire paycheck on a new evening gown or dinner jacket with lapels cut to reflect this season's fashion. Only a spouse can legitimately claim to be mortified by what you wear or consequently to suffer months of public humiliation afterward.

The Missing Movie Escort

Once you have gotten over the idea that every Big Event calls for a Big Date, you may find that you can enjoy attending a lot of them alone. In any case, you will sometimes need to go by yourself to such places as the movies or the theater, or miss seeing Meryl Streep for the second time in a row. If you're still a little shy about handing over a single ticket, one useful trick is to go to a place you associate with couples, but to go there at a time when fewer will be present. If you've never gone alone to the movies, for example, go during the day on a weekday, not on a weekend. Duck out of work early or take a long lunch hour to reward yourself for finishing a big project. One single woman, who took in a movie on a midweek afternoon, uncomfortably found herself seated next to a man whom she discovered to be playing with more than the popcorn. After that, she made it a point always to sit on an aisle seat, thereby reducing by fifty percent the odds that the seat next to her would be occupied by someone similar—and increasing the ease with which she could inform an usher if it was.

If it's not a movie you're pining to go to, but a play or concert, you might attend a Wednesday matinee instead of an evening performance. Most single people work so hard at their jobs that a few instances of this sort of playing hooky couldn't begin to pay them back for all the overtime they have logged. (And that, incidentally, is partly why you won't find a chapter on work in this book—the chances are good that you are doing far too much already and don't need anybody to urge you to do any more.) The nice part of going to Wednesday matinees is that their costs are often lower than what you would pay on a weekend, and you also won't be surrounded by couples but by club women from the suburbs. And what do you care if you are seen alone by the entire Scarsdale PTA?

"So How Come You're Not Married?"

Whatever activities you engage in, on your own or paired up, you're likely to encounter questions that married people wouldn't, and you had best be prepared for them. Only family members and close friends used to believe they had a right to make inquiries such as: "So how come you're not married?" These also tended to be made mostly at weddings at which a half dozen of your cousins paraded about in matching pastel-colored dresses that made them look like Sno Cones with feet.

Today, you get asked why you're not married by strangers you meet in bus terminals—and it is rarely sufficient merely to laugh hysterically in reply. Neither is it considered good manners to point out that nobody asks married couples: "So how come you're not divorced?"

No doubt about it: most people still consider a single person's marital status to be fair game for impertinent questions. And never *mind* what they ask about your sex life: Masters and Johnson should only have gotten up the nerve to ask such questions of the subjects that made them so famous.

The most important thing is simply to remember that you are never obliged to reply to such questions in the same sort of detail that went into the personal essay that accompanied your college applications. Questions about your sex life are probably best answered by changing the subject to something more interesting, such as the Eastern Division playoffs. Common decency dictates that married couples not be asked about their sex lives, so why shouldn't you claim the same privilege?

Your best bet for dealing with queries about why you haven't married is to work out a light reply in keeping with your sense of humor. Most people have grown a little tired of hearing that "marriage is a great institution, but who wants to live in an institution," so it's probably best to steer clear of that one. And it takes a lot of pizzazz to get away with saying that you agree with Groucho Marx ("Marriage is the chief cause of divorce") or with Zsa Zsa Gabor ("A man is incomplete until he's married—and then he's finished"). But most single people *can* manage cheerily to insist: "Well, nobody's ever made me an offer I couldn't refuse," or "Oh, I couldn't possibly get married—it would cut into my social life."

The new technologies of our age have inspired other responses that would have been unthinkable until recently. One young woman swears that she tells her mother she doesn't need to be married because she's having herself cloned, and a single man has been known to claim that he has "a NOW account at the sperm bank." Of course, one highly effective answer to a question about why you haven't married works no less well today than it ever did: "Just lucky, I guess."

And now a few words about some problems that you can't always dismiss with a snappy one-liner or two:

Loneliness

The best definition I have read of loneliness is the poet May Sarton's observation that people are lonely when they have no one with whom to exchange the deepest part of themselves. I like her words partly because they explain why marriage offers no warranty against loneliness: you can have been married to someone for years and still not be able to share your thoughts and feelings with that person. Sarton's definition also helps to explain why single people need not suffer from a lifetime of loneliness: you can be unmarried and still be able to share your thoughts and feelings fully with others.

It probably goes without saying that the amount of time you spend alone has little to do with whether or not you will feel lonely. In living alone, I've always found that the hours I spend by myself help me to understand what I want to express to others. Without private time, I tend to lose sight of myself. In conversation, I begin to hear myself echoing the ideas of others, whether or not I agree—an experience that can be both lonely and depressing. (Who *is* she, I ask, this person who so easily grafts onto herself the ideas and mannerisms of other people?) So the hours I spend alone are less the times that make me feel lonely than the times that keep me from feeling lonely, by allowing me to tap again into an essential self that I can later share with others. And this, I suspect, helps to explain why I have rarely felt lonely during the time I have been single.

Nor am I alone in enjoying time by myself. Not long ago, two researchers reviewed more than twenty-seven thousand questionnaires on intimacy and loneliness in America and published their findings in *In Search of Intimacy* (Delacorte, 1982). Carin Rubenstein and Phillip Shaver concluded that single people with close ties to others were usually no lonelier than married ones. The key, they found, lay in learning how to obtain those ties without a spouse.

The people who continue to forge deep bonds to others throughout their lives need not fear that they will still be lonely in their old age. Rubenstein and Shaver found, to the contrary, that the loneliest Americans were adolescents and young adults, under twenty-five. Indeed, the older people grew, the better equipped they often seemed to be to ward off emotional isolation, perhaps because their survival skills in general were simply better. One researcher, who interviewed unmarried elderly people in Detroit, found that the men and women who had remained single for a lifetime were no less enthusiastic about their lives than were the divorced or widowed. In fact, they valued their independence and were glad, at their age, not to have to worry about anybody else.

What if you feel—in spite of all that you've read about how being alone doesn't have to mean being lonely—that you are still too isolated for comfort? The best approach is usually to try to relieve your symptoms and then to work on their underlying causes. Make a little list of clubs you've heard about or classes you might like to take, then call or write for information about them. Have a Sunday afternoon open house and invite everybody on your floor or the other people around your own age in your apartment building. Set up a little schedule for yourself that requires you to have a minimum number of conversations and meetings with friends every week, and plan for them in advance. (Plan, for instance, to call at least one person every night for a chat, and to have at least one weekly lunch with a friend you haven't seen in a while.) These short-term measures can help you feel better while you are attempting to work out a long-range solution to feelings of emotional emptiness.

A more lasting solution often begins with simply making more of an effort to talk about your feelings with others. You may feel lonely, paradoxically, because you have no one to talk to about your loneliness. And simply bringing your feelings out into the open can lead to the discovery that you aren't nearly so alone as you think. A separated woman told me that, after months of feeling bereft, she finally summoned up the courage to tell a friend that she had been at loose ends since her husband moved out. Would it be possible, she asked, for the two of them to see each other more often? The woman told me her friend's response had been unequivocal: "Of course we can get together—and thank goodness you asked! I've been thinking about you a lot and have been frankly a little worried about your turning down offers of help." The conversation turned out to be a watershed for both people. The separated woman felt better for having said aloud what she'd been thinking, and her friend was flattered and happy that she'd been the one to be taken into confidence.

As their experience suggests, one key to relieving loneliness lies in a willingness to reach out instead of waiting for others to reach out to you. Many studies have shown that most lonely people do not have deeply rooted psychological problems. Neither are they unattractive ones who have little to offer others. Rather, they are men and women who are unwilling to take the first step: to make the first phone call, to pay the first compliment, or to issue the first invitation for dinner or drinks. Lonely people also tend to be men and women who, although sometimes willing to take that first step, are often unwilling to follow through: to keep making overtures to maintain communication with people they know. Research has shown that lonely people tend to be especially sensitive to real or imagined rejection—to be the sort who interpret neutral or even positive comments as negative ones, or who will never issue a second invitation once a first has been declined.

It's rarely a bad idea, in any case, to sit down with someone who has a lot of friends and to ask how he or she has made them. You may need to be more creative in how you connect with others. I recently read a charming newspaper column about two young lawyers, both roommates who moved to my city knowing only one other person. Too busy to join a lot of groups but still wanting to get to know people, they asked their one friend to dinner—and asked her to bring several friends whom she thought they'd like to meet. One of the invited friends admitted that it had at first felt odd to be asked to dinner at the apartment of someone she had never met. But she wound up having a wonderful time, admiring the young lawyers' spunk and imagination, and planning to have them over to her place soon. More single people need to respond in such a refreshingly down-to-earth way to the loneliness they feel.

Single-Parent Traps

Although feelings of isolation can afflict anybody, single parents often suffer from them especially acutely. It's hard enough to order your own life without the aid and comfort of a spouse; it can take everything you've got to try also to manage the life of a child. I sometimes think that if there are two major groups of single people—those who enlisted and those who got drafted—the ones who ought to get combat pay are single parents.

Being a single parent generally means having all of the responsibilities that other unattached people do, but with fewer freedoms and more financial problems. Then again, widespread divorce is still such a relatively new phenomenon that a lot is still unknown about how children react to it.

One consequence is that single parents need to be especially inventive in how they come to terms with their own lives. And few can manage without a little advice from others in the same boat. Many weekly or alternative newspapers carry classified ads listing support groups for divorced men and women, with or without custody of their children. Some adult-ed centers and YMCAs or YWCAs are home to similar organizations or can tell you where to find one. If you can't find a group in your area, or haven't been happy with the ones you've turned up, you might form your own by putting up bulletin-board notices or taking out an ad in the personals column of a magazine or newspaper.

You may also be able to do a lot even without a formal support group. One single mother I know was dismayed by the off-again, on-again visits of her ex-husband. He continually raised his children's hopes of seeing him, then dashed them by failing to show up at the last minute. Wanting nonetheless to make sure that her children would be able to rely on adults, their mother decided to rent a beach house in Westhampton annually with several other single parents. The shared cottage gave all of the children a familiar place to return to each summer, with the same faces inside it. The parents benefited from the arrangement no less than did their children, who over the years came to regard their summer playmates as their unofficial cousins.

Depression

Everybody, married or single, occasionally feels a little low. But how can you tell whether your own sinking moments are all that much worse than anybody else's?

Most mental health experts see red flags when people clearly manifest their distress by losing or gaining weight, ceasing to care about their appearance, developing insomnia, becoming listless and lacking in energy, or expressing feelings of hopelessness about the future. And you always enter a danger zone when depression begins to interfere with your ability to function, either at work or at home. Do you find yourself calling in sick when you aren't or holing up in your apartment because you can't face even your dearest friends? Don't let your suffering go on and lead to consequences far worse, for you and everybody you're close to.

How can you find the right kind of help when you need it? The experts are always saying, "Consult your family physician." The problem when you are single is that you will often have no such thing or have one but find that he or she is thousands of miles away. Maybe you can get a referral from your internist or a friend. I would also seek referrals from clergy or call the local Family Service Association for leads. Don't let the word "family" throw you; this venerable organization has for years been providing referrals to qualified counselors, for married and single people alike. A local FSA office might also offer seminars on such subjects as becoming a single parent or banishing the holiday blues. You may also want to call the nearest chapter of your state Psychological Association, listed in the phone book under the name of your state or to get in touch with the psychiatry department at a nearby teaching hospital. Ask, especially, about the newer short-term courses of treatment, often called "brief therapies," that can help you work on a specific problem over a finite period. Not everybody needs to spend years on the couch to overcome a psychological problem that might be readily amenable to treatment by other means.

It's also important to weigh any counselor's advice against your own perceptions. Psychotherapy has become so fashionable that single people can overuse it as often as underuse it. When I lived in Manhattan, I knew any number of single women who were forever being told by their psychiatrists that the reason they couldn't form deep relations with men was that they were secretly "afraid" of "intimacy." Yet anybody who hadn't been declared legally blind could have seen that another reason some couldn't form those relations was that in New York single women outnumber single men approximately the way the Indians outnumbered Custer. Another reason they couldn't find dates was that their therapy sessions were eating up all the money they could have been spending on such things as videodating service memberships or trips to Europe, either of which might have done more to broaden their lives than months of sessions on the couch.

Although therapy has its place, so do hard work and common sense, combined with a working sense of humor about things you can't control. So don't neglect any of those. A reporter once asked Woody Allen if his life had changed since he had become famous. "Yes," he replied. "Now that I'm better known, I strike out with a better class of women." Exactly. Solve the problems that you have now and you may find yourself confronted by others that follow in their wake. So the trick is to learn to roll with them, like steering into a skid, instead of always berating yourself for having a life that has flaws.

Overeating and Overdrinking

Although food and alcohol abuse are so closely related to depression that they might appear inseparable, they deserve a short section of their own for at least two reasons. One is that compulsive eating and drinking are two of the most insidious problems that can ail you when you are single, because they can creep up on you softly. Even if you've never had a weight or alcohol problem, it's easy to ravish a bottle of wine or pint of Godiva ice cream on an empty Saturday night. Let too many of those nights roll around, and you may be in real trouble.

The good news is that food and alcohol abuse often respond quite well to forms of treatment other than psychotherapy. Not many psychiatrists have cured more compulsive drinkers than the local chapter of Alcoholics Anonymous. And few have so impressive a record of treating foodaholics as does Overeaters Anonymous, a terrific organization that uses the principles of AA to help compulsive eaters. (Check your phone book for the chapter of either that's nearest you, and remember that all inquiries are always kept confidential.) Apart from OA, many other organizations have outstanding track records of helping people lose weight. They include Weight Watchers, Lean Line, Diet Center, and TOPS (an acronym for Take Off Pounds Sensibly). All such groups have a particular benefit for single men and women: their staff members and other participants can supply the sort of moral support for a diet that married people get from their spouses.

Whether you want to cut back on food or on alcohol, you might also consider going to a health spa that offers a low-calorie, liquor-free diet. A good guide to sixty-three health resorts, in the United States and elsewhere, is *The Spa Book* (Crown, 1983), by Judy Babcock and Judy Kennedy. See if you can find it at your bookstore or library. Like diet clubs, spa vacations allow you to connect easily with other people who share your goals and whose encouragement could help you reach them.

Crime

Singlehood often entails its own rites of passage: getting your first apartment, making your first trip to Europe, or celebrating the holidays for the first time without your parents. Too many single people discover that one of the rites of passage can be surviving your first burglary or getting your pocket picked for the first time. FBI statistics show that single people of both sexes are more likely than married ones to become victims of virtually every sort of crime, although law enforcement officials aren't entirely sure why. One possible explanation is that single people often live alone and are therefore more vulnerable to all sorts of dangers. Single people can also be less careful than others. They stay out late and don't take taxis home. They go away on vacation without putting timers on their lights. They leave parties with strangers whose last names they barely know. Is there any way a single man or woman can *ever* be really safe?

Perhaps no more than any married one can. But, after years of living alone, I've worked out a set of safety guidelines that seem to have reduced my chances of becoming a victim, and police officers have confirmed that they can work for others.

For starters, I walk briskly and purposefully on all streets, especially at night. I also cross a street immediately if I suspect I am being followed. (This, a police officer once told me, at least lets someone else know that you are aware of being followed; an even better idea is to cross the street suddenly and reverse your direction, and then if you are still being followed, scream.) I always have my keys out before I get to my apartment and never stand in a vestibule fumbling for them in my purse. Late at night I always take a cab home, tip the taxi driver extravagantly, after asking him or her to wait in front of my building until I am safely inside.

I also make it a point to try to live in a building that hasn't been broken into in anybody's memory. Ask other tenants about this before you move in. After years of signing leases, I've found that some buildings are simply easier marks for criminals than others. Vulnerable buildings that get broken into tend to do so more than once. One that's never been

broken into—for whatever reason—seems unlikely to become a target. I also avoid living on a fire escape, unless it
leads to high-walled courtyards impenetrable from the
street.

Wherever I live, I never simply buzz in a visitor but go
downstairs and see who's there or check out the person
through a peephole. Finally, I have an unpublished phone
number—and not just because I have found that it drastically reduces your chances of getting obscene phone calls.
Nearly everybody I know who's had his or her apartment
broken into has first gotten a series of calls from someone
checking to see whether or not anyone was home. (Burglars
apparently copy your name off your buzzer, then just go
look you up in the phone book, something they can do easily
if your name appears on the outside of your building.) Many
intruders, of course, won't show up if you're around. But
just knowing that someone *could* find out if I'm home always makes me feel vulnerable—a problem my answering
machine doesn't relieve. With an unlisted phone number, I
am spared the harmless crank calls as well as the possibly
less innocent ones.

Illness

Sickness, like crime, is something you hope never to have
to deal with at all. Illness is no joke even when you are
married. Get sick when you are single and you may feel as
though you've suddenly been visited by every disaster that
Indiana Jones somehow missed inside the Temple of Doom.

Let me suggest, however, that an illness may not be so
bad as what it often seems to represent. Any ailment you
get when single tends to make concrete your deepest fears
and longings. It seems to give you permission to feel sorry
for yourself for not being married and to believe your life
would be far better if you were. Then you'd have somebody
to take care of you, and not just in illness. The same sorts of
bleak feelings can arise when you are healthy but they tend

to be a little easier to brush aside, because there's less reason for indulging them. The result is that, when you do get sick, lots of long-buried feelings about singlehood can come tumbling out unexpectedly.

But there is a catch to feeling sorry for yourself for being single instead of feeling sorry for yourself because you're sick—and it is that it can keep you from doing something to make yourself better. Singlehood, after all, is something you can't be immediately cured of, so you may be tempted to let yourself suffer. Illness you might be cured of quite quickly, but not if you pity yourself to a point that you won't even ask for help from your friends. Asking for that help is therefore the first thing you need to do to make yourself feel better, not just in illness, but about being single, too.

A lot of single people begin to worry obsessively about what might happen if they got sick with something worse than flu, which is never a question to take lightly. In a funny way, though, large illnesses can be a lot easier to deal with than small ones. When a big illness strikes, people gather round you in ways they don't when little ones flare up. Then again, you have options during a major affliction that you don't have during a minor one. If you were really sick, you could move back in with your parents until you had recovered. Or you could stay in a hospital or get a private nurse to come in. When you have only a minor problem, you are essentially going it alone, and that is precisely the problem.

The trick, then, is not to worry about the big disasters that may never happen but to do what you can to protect yourself should they ever turn up without warning. Above all, obtain as much health insurance as you can, whether you pay for it or someone else does. Try to get a policy that provides a million dollars' worth of coverage. Unbelievable as it sounds, even a quarter or a half million dollars may not be enough if you come down with something serious. A man hospitalized with AIDS recently incurred ninety-eight thousand dollars' worth of medical expenses in a mere three months. After ex-baseball star Tony Conigliaro suffered a

massive heart attack, he required medical care that cost
nearly a quarter of a million dollars in one year—and forced
his former Red Sox teammates to hold a fund raiser to help
out his family. So don't kid yourself into thinking that you're
young and strong and won't get sick. Healthy or not, you
can still be the victim of a brutal crime or a hit-and-run
accident that can leave you—or your family—penniless if
you aren't covered.

Most health and major medical policies, put together, will
cover about eighty percent of all your medical expenses for
a serious illness, after you have paid a deductible. Even
paying the remaining twenty percent, however, can run to
thousands, if you require surgery or an otherwise prolonged
hospital stay. If you're concerned about being able to meet
such costs, you may want to buy a supplemental health
insurance policy, known as an "excess major medical plan,"
that will cover everything your other plans don't. (Their
deductible is the amount paid out by your other insurance
companies first.) Ask whether you can buy this sort of coverage through your employer, or consult an independent
agent. Remember, too, that if the bottom really drops out
and you get sick enough to exhaust all your savings, you may
still be able to declare yourself indigent and become eligible for Medicaid.

The Ultimate

Grim and heartless as it is of me to bring this up in a book
that is supposed to be about the *joy* of being single, you not
only could get sick, depressed, lonely, or mugged when you
are unmarried, you could even die or suffer from illness so
catastrophic that it leaves you hovering somewhere pre-
cariously between life and death. What are the implications
of either of those facts?

First, if you are a single man or woman without children
and die without a will, everything you own will go to your
parents or, if they are deceased, to your brothers and sisters,

followed by other relatives in a progression spelled out by the intestacy laws of your state. Thus, nothing would go to your friends or to a lover, even to a live-in one. So you especially need to have a will drawn up if you would like people in either of those categories to inherit some of your assets. At the very least you need a handwritten letter of intent spelling out exactly what you'd like to happen to your belongings if you were to die. Nothing guarantees that a court—or your parents—will honor a document not properly drawn up by a lawyer. But a handwritten letter can spell out guidelines that a loving family might be willing to heed and so is still better than nothing.

Most single people put off drawing up a will either because they believe they have too few assets to leave to anyone or because they don't know whom to select as the executor of their estate. This reasoning tends to overlook the fact that, even if your possessions have slight monetary value, they almost always have a sentimental importance that wouldn't go unappreciated by your friends. A will lets you acknowledge that, in however small a way. The author Lillian Hellman, who was divorced early in life and never remarried, left a substantial estate when she died in 1984. Apart from her financial bequests, she also stipulated in her will that certain close friends would be able to pick one item apiece from among her possessions—something other single people could do, too. The writer Mignon McLaughlin has said that any woman who wants to achieve immortalilty should leave each item of jewelry she owns to a different young friend or relative. And anchorwoman Jessica Savitch, who died unmarried, had made a will that reportedly left one third of her estate to her mother, one third to a sister, and one third to be divided among seven close acquaintances.

Most people select a family member or trusted friend to be the executor of their estate. But if you aren't close to your family and don't want to assign the job to someone you know well, you can name as your executor the lawyer who drew up your will. Many bank officers also serve this function for their clients. If you're interested in having one do the same for you, ask about this service where you have your checking account or at the nearest office of any large bank. Another good idea is to name a friend and a bank or law firm to be coexecutors, which divides up the work.

Don't be deterred by the belief that drawing up a will has to cost a lot. Most states now have no-frills legal clinics that will do one under one hundred dollars, leaving you with a document no less valid than one that costs more. Among the better-known clinics are those run by St. Louis-based Hyatt Legal Services and by Jacoby and Meyers, which started in Los Angeles. Both companies have offices in many states.

It's also worth thinking about what you'd want to happen if you became critically ill and unable to make decisions about your own care. If you wouldn't want those decisions to be made by your parents or siblings, you need to have a legal document drawn up assigning that function to somebody else. The same is true if you are separated but not divorced and want to assign that function to someone other than your spouse. You can also have a statement drawn up giving power of attorney over your finances, in the event of an incapacitating illness, to someone you designate. You may also want to have a lawyer draw up a so-called "living will" that specifies when you'd like to have life-support systems withdrawn in the event of a catastrophic illness. All too often, married people discuss such matters with their spouses, but single people talk about them with no one, with consequences that can be tragic.

Finally, don't stint on life insurance just because you are young and single. The financial planners who tell single people to carry just enough to cover their burial expenses are frankly *crazy*. The biggest risk in waiting until you marry to buy a lot of life insurance is that by then you may have developed a health problem that could severely restrict your ability to obtain as much coverage as you'd like. Another risk is that you could die unexpectedly, having left virtually nothing to the parents or siblings you love. If even one person would be psychologically devastated by your death, that is reason enough to carry a policy naming that person as the beneficiary. A large life-insurance check could help that person get back on his or her feet, by whatever means are necessary, in the wake of a terrible emotional blow. The money would also provide the sort of financial safety net that a loan from you would provide if you were alive. Check into the many sorts of policies available through your employer, credit union, credit-card issuers, or savings bank if you live in a state that offers savings-bank life insurance. At least one of those institutions ought to be able to sell you a generous but affordable policy that might someday become the nicest thing you ever did for somebody you care about desperately.

Trust in the Pendulum

Does that list cover all of the disasters that could befall you when you are single? Of course not. Yet you may suffer none of them while you are single, so you have reason to hope for the best while being prepared for the worst.

Remember, too, that when you are single your marital status can be only one of several things seemingly working against you. You may also be young, poor, and living in a city in which you know practically no one. Perhaps you are locked into emotional hand-to-hand combat with your parents, who are resisting your independence at every bend in the road. Or maybe you are newly divorced and a refugee from a court battle that has left you with your home in someone else's hands, your savings decimated, and your children spending three nights a week with a person in whose eyes you have become a reincarnation of Rasputin, Boss Tweed, and Jack the Ripper rolled into one.

The most important thing, if any of those apply, is to try to suspend apocalyptic judgments about their long-term effects. Trust instead in the tendency of a pendulum to swing back to its point of origin. If you felt emotionally strong before, you'll feel that way again. And in the meantime one of the best things you can do for yourself is to keep yourself physically strong. Step up your exercise routine; join a health club; take up a new sport or two. An hour of working out a day can sometimes do more for you than an hour on the couch each day.

My own experience suggests that you can generally count on a roughly two-year recovery period from a major upheaval, such as a divorce or transplanting to a new city, and you can sometimes require longer. In the interim, if you aren't unrelentingly miserable, your comfort level definitely tends to fluctuate within the subnormal zone.

Interestingly, though, the times that come after the bleaker ones often will be among your best, because it can take a major uprooting to rid you of destructive patterns you couldn't have shed any other way. All of the clichés you've heard about the highest mountains coming out of the sea are—in a sense—true. Chiseled into the stone over the entrance to my college library were the words: "You shall know the truth, and the truth shall make you free." Not until many years after graduation did someone kindly advise me of its corollary: "The truth shall make you free, but first it shall make you miserable."

I would never have written this book had I not been kicked and pummeled toward it, until I was made practically black and blue and bleeding from the throat by the most difficult period of my adult life—a time in which my life sank so low that I could never decide whether to call Dial-a-Joke or Dial-a-Prayer, given that the former seemed to be what my life had become and the latter appeared to be what it no longer had. It took months for me to be able to climb out of bed in the morning without believing that the Four Horsemen of the Apocalypse would ring my buzzer by 11 A.M. Until then, I identified with the Doonesbury cartoon in which a friend says "Good morning" to Zonker Harris, who replies: "That's fine for *you* to say."

The worst part of it was that, the more I tried to help myself, the unhappier I often felt, because my efforts seemed to be going nowhere. The best I could manage to do was to try to influence the few things I did have control over. I ate right, bought an exercise bicycle, moved to a sunnier apartment, and rented a summer place on Martha's Vineyard. I also saw friends, got a little professional help, and, most of all, continued to get up and work, on this book and other projects, every day.

I wish I could say that a cataclysmic breakthrough occurred to change my life for the better. I even wish I could say that something I did proved to be the turning point. But neither of those was true. What happened was simply that, little by little, things got better. I might not have been able to change things as quickly as I wanted, but at least I didn't make myself worse. I just allowed circumstances to work *for* me, where they might have worked against me.

What happened to me, and what will likely happen to you, is that the pendulum did swing back, leaving me stronger for the experiences I'd had while it was moving. Like Pogo, I had seemed to be confronted by "insurmountable opportunities." But once I began to recognize them for the challenges they were—and not problems I could get out of by something so clear-cut as getting married—they began to become manageable. The professional advice I got helped, but so did lots of other things, including help from my friends. As Karen Horney once remarked, and most of us learn eventually: "Fortunately, psychotherapy is not the only answer. Life itself remains a very effective therapist."

11

Jingle Bell Blues and the Heartbreak of Hanukkah: A Holiday Survival Strategy

One of the bleakest moments I have faced as a single adult didn't occur after the breakup of my longest-playing love affair, after an important job fell out from under me, or after I got a 102° fever and was too weak even to call a friend. The terrible hour arose instead during the parade of tall ships that appeared in New York Harbor as part of the country's bicentennial celebration, on July 4, 1976, when I was living alone in a small studio apartment in Manhattan.

Deeply immersed in a magazine article I had been writing, I had made no plans to watch the procession of two- and three-masted boats that the media had been hyping for weeks. Having long since wearied of stores filled with Liberty Bell cookie jars and cars bedecked with red, white, and blue bumper stickers, I'd decided I'd had my fill of bicentennial hoopla. Besides, my article seemed far more interesting than looking at a bunch of old ships that would only be shown later on TV.

That, at least, was what I believed, until I decided to interrupt my work briefly to stroll over to a bank of the

Hudson River, on the brilliantly sunny day that the Fourth had turned out to be. Along the shores of the river were more people than I had ever seen in one place—all seemingly in groups of two or more. I saw straight couples, gay couples, and golden-age couples watching the procession from lawn chairs. I also saw families, including one in which a mother had dressed her two sons up like mini-George Washingtons, in three-cornered hats, knee breeches, and ruffled white shirts.

It took only minutes before I began to feel more alone than I had ever felt and less because I wasn't part of a couple than because I wasn't with anybody at all. Like John Kennedy's assassination and the first time men walked on the moon, the parade of tall ships seemed meant to be shared. But I couldn't even call a friend from a pay phone and ask him or her to meet me at the river, because everybody I knew had already arranged to view the spectacle with someone else.

The best I could do was simply to try to store up memories of the event to share with others later, which seemed a poor substitute for having a friend at my side. Back in my apartment, I took another look at the event on TV, in the company only of Walter Cronkite. And even he was a little teary, though not for the same reason I was.

Looking back on that event in subsequent years, I have come to see it as the beginning of an important lesson: celebrating holidays with loved ones makes most people feel as though they are really living. But single men and women often find it hard to do that when their nearest and dearest aren't at hand.

Some large cities have recently begun to sprout groups that exist for no other reason than to unite single people at holidays. These organizations consist of unattached men and women who get together for communal dinners on Thanksgiving, Passover, and other occasions, and perhaps they represent an idea worthy of wider consideration. But

I'm not so sure. Is it really an improvement to substitute singles-only get-togethers for families-only ones?

I have always found that singles-only groups can be just as dreary as married-only ones, at the holidays or at any other time. So the new groups seem best viewed as stopgap measures—good, let's say, for single people who have just moved to a new city or recently become separated—and not as a long-term solution.

There seems no getting around the fact that Americans have always viewed holidays and other special occasions as family times, and to feel part of them, you need to have connections to a group bound by blood as much as by need. Not to have such ties can leave you feeling as though you are denying the ostrich egg lying squarely in your path instead of looking at it head on and dying it purple for Easter.

One good way to forge those connections is simply to make more effort to incorporate other people's families into your own. Most happy single people get adopted by one or more older or better-established couples, preferably with children. Once you, too, have done so, you will always have friends willing to take you in when it matters most, just as you take them in at other times.

Until you find a group of such spiritual kinfolk, I believe you need to look special events squarely in the eye. Often it helps to mention your lack of plans to a clergy member, who may be able to put you in touch with a family in his or her congregation that would be happy to set an extra holiday plate. Another good idea is to make a call to the International House for foreign students at the college nearest you. Many of these residences for undergraduates from abroad prepare elaborate holiday feasts for men and women who can't afford to go home for the events. You may be able to join in them by offering to help. Or how about inviting a foreign student or two to *your* home? Alternately, you might get in touch with one of the thirty or so nationwide branches of the International Institute, an organization that aims to help the foreign-born feel at home in this country. Any of these, too, may serve up gala holiday meals to help introduce people to American traditions, and you may be able to participate simply by joining the institute. A double benefit often results, in fact, from connecting with people from other countries. Single people and foreign visitors or transplants have a particular affinity for each other because both are, in a sense, outsiders—single people in a married society and people from other countries in an American one. This often means that the people you celebrate the holidays with may become good friends for other times, too.

Yet it doesn't really matter whom you admit your needs to, so much as that you bring them up with somebody. Any number of otherwise quite sensible single men and women would sooner confess to shoplifting than to facing a Christmas or Thanksgiving alone. Asked about their holiday plans, they finesse the question—or, worse, lie outright, saying that they expect to be visiting relatives in Sioux Falls, when they know perfectly well that they may visit with no one but their doormen.

This sort of dissembling can be a tragic mistake, and not just because it leaves you feeling something less than honest. By denying your desire to spend the holidays with somebody else, you virtually insure that you'll spend them alone—or at least in a less grand style than might otherwise be possible. Somebody whose holiday table is already crowded with out-of-town guests might still love to have you over for an after-dinner drink. But nobody can invite you for anything without knowing you are available.

It seems most single people fail to speak up when they are alone at the holidays partly because they fear that others will feel sorry for them. The idea apparently is that the measure of your holidays is the measure of your life—that the holiday, in a sense, *represents* your whole life. This, of course, is just silly. Just as good people can have occasional bad days or even bad years, so can they have a bad holiday or two, without having anyone think less of them for it.

More than that, it is never what you say, so much as how you say it, that determines others' reactions to it. I have known people about to have their heads shaved for brain surgery who manifested such unrelenting optimism that you almost wanted to take a razor to your own scalp to discover what made them so cheerful. I have known others who faced the removal of a wisdom tooth with such gloom and foreboding that, had you not known otherwise, you would have felt sure they were about to undergo a triple coronary bypass at the hands of a local meat butcher. At holiday times, you can display a similar range of emotions. You can talk about your lack of Thanksgiving plans with such despair that friends will wonder whether to slip the number of a crisis hot line into your "In" box at work. Or you can show such good-natured grace that your kith will marvel that you haven't begun accepting sealed, competitive bids for the pleasure of your company. One single woman realized that she couldn't go home for both Christmas and Thanksgiving, and so chose the former. As Thanksgiving approached, and no invitations to other tables materialized, she admitted to a coworker: "I'll really miss being with my family over the holiday. This is the first time my only Thanksgiving companion will be the Bullwinkle float in the Macy's parade." Her disarming candor almost immediately resulted in an invitation to drop by the home of someone in her office, who said he'd had no idea that someone so personable would not already have a half dozen invitations in hand. Without actually inviting yourself to anyone's house for the day, it is nonetheless quite possible to advertise your availability with a question such as: "Do you have any idea what single people in this city tend to do on holidays? I'm still so new here that I have no idea where other people like me go when they can't go home."

The other good way to insure that you will always have a family with whom to spend a holiday is to share your favorite rituals and traditions with the people you like best. Nobody needs to mark every national or other holiday, but everybody does need to celebrate some. Make a point of honoring the days that mean the most to you, either because you always treated them specially in childhood, or simply because you always wished that you had.

Here are some of the ways to make specific holidays memorable:

The Fourth of July

What holiday could be more appropriate for single men and women to mark than Independence Day? Journalist Betsy Wade has written that her family marks the event by reading aloud the Declaration of Independence—something you and your single friends might do, too. (Read the words out of your almanac or pass out parchment reproductions of the document, available in many drug and stationery stores.) You might also orchestrate a tailgate picnic to be held at the site of the nearest fireworks display. I once shepherded some sixteen people across Manhattan via subway to watch fireworks being shot off over the Hudson River. Each guest invited to the party brought a culinary contribution, such as a cake etched with an icing firecracker or a red, blue, and "white" fruit salad made with strawberries, blueberries, and pineapple.

St. Patrick's Day

Chicagoans dye their river green for the day. Bostonians pack the local Irish pubs. And New Yorkers watch the Rolls-Royce of parades—an event for which the white stripe down Fifth Avenue used to be painted green.

If you have always loved such displays of Gaelic pride, why not stage your own? Give a small dinner party at which you serve corned beef and cabbage, washed down by steaming mugs of Irish coffee. (To make it: add a teaspoon of sugar and one and a half ounces of Irish whiskey, such as Jameson's, to a tulip-shaped wineglass; fill with strong, freshly brewed coffee and a dollop of whipped cream.) I make instead a huge pot of Irish stew, using the recipe in my ever faithful *Joy of Cooking,* and invite friends to drop by after work for a bowlful. I also serve loaves of Irish soda bread from a bakery and frosty glasses of Guinness Stout or Bailey's Irish Cream. Traditional Irish folk tunes waft from my stereo, and one year I devised an Irish trivia quiz and awarded green bagels as a prize. Were my apartment not big enough for dinner parties, I might instead buy several tickets for an Irish folk music or dance performance and invite my friends to join me at it.

Thanksgiving

One unmarried friend told me her life felt as though it had bottomed out on the Thanksgiving Day when her mid-day meal consisted of a cold turkey sandwich from a deli— an experience she might have avoided by inviting a single friend from another city to spend the holiday with her. Even if you're going away for the holiday, you may be able to heighten your enjoyment of it by having a small celebration on the Monday or Tuesday before the event. Serve a sexy alternative to the usual bird: maybe rock Cornish hens or turkey breast Marsala. (Adapt a chicken or veal recipe calling for the same wine.) One divorced man invites his friends over early in Thanksgiving week for a simple meal of pumpkin or cranberry bread and cheese. Afterward, all of the guests sing Thanksgiving hymns as he plunks out their tunes on his aging Chickering baby grand, and all of them finish with a lusty chorus of "Over the River and Through the Woods."

Easter and Passover

In my household, Easter wouldn't be Easter without church services on Sunday morning. Sometimes I serve a traditional Easter breakfast, consisting of ham and hot cross buns, for a friend or two. If the weather is good, we might take in the local Easter parade afterward. Another woman gives an annual Easter Eve dinner the night before the holiday. She asks each guest to bring one Easter egg, candy or the real thing, that goes into a basket to form a center-piece for her table. You could do the same thing and give each guest a foil-wrapped chocolate egg as a favor. Alter-nately, go with a group of friends to hear the Easter portion of Handel's "Messiah" at a church or concert hall.

If you celebrate Passover, why not go to a family seder the first night and make one for your friends on the second? Add their special concerns to the prayers and have fun deciding which grown-up will assume the role of the youn-gest child, who gets to ask the traditional Passover question, "What makes this night different from all others?" Better still, get your friends to bring along their children so you don't have to appoint a stand-in.

Christmas, Hanukkah, and— oh, God—New Year's Eve

December is the cruelest month for single people. Almost nobody can get through it without regularly bumping into parents buying toys for their children, newlyweds heading off to visit a set of in-laws, or couples marking their engage-ment with a diamond big enough to do permanent damage to the cornea. Every gift and card shop you visit can seem to remind you that even Santa Claus is supposed to have a Mrs. Claus. Worst of all, just when the month is about to end and you think you can be done with it comes the killer: New Year's Eve.

Jingle bell blues *can* be cured, but not by trying to dupli-cate line by line the traditions of your married friends. Their lives are usually just too different from yours to offer much inspiration. Instead, think back to the rituals you par-ticularly enjoyed during your own childhood or that you would like to enjoy now, and adapt them to your needs and interests.

Nothing can make you feel more happily connected to the holidays, for instance, than having a tree. But many single people's apartments are far too small for a six-foot evergreen, and who wants to lug one up four flights, anyway? Instead, you might substitute a potted Alberta spruce or similar tree, just big enough for a tabletop. Decorate it with small silvery ornaments about an inch or so in diameter or with lots of pretty bows. Any good flower shop can make one of these tabletop trees for you, complete with all the trimmings, so that all you need to do is pick it up on your way home from the office.

Another idea is to decorate your *Ficus benjaminus* or another big tree or plant. Or tie red ribbons around the pots of all your plants and describe them to your friends as your "surrogate Christmas trees." In the absence of any other holiday greenery, a red or white poinsettia plant can make a whole room spring to life. Set one inside a wicker basket and place it inside your fireplace opening, or put one on each side of it. And, whether or not you actually have a Christmas tree on the premises, burning a balsam- or pine-scented candle can make your apartment smell as though you do.

If you have the room and the energy to put up a real tree, try to personalize it. A lot of single people haven't yet acquired a collection of ornaments with real emotional significance. But it is easier than might be expected to come by these quickly.

One way to personalize a tree is to have an annual tree-trimming party to which you ask each guest to bring an ornament. Do this for several years running and you won't just have established your first holiday tradition: you'll have an evergreen more attractive than that of many married couples you know. (Be sure to keep lists of who gave which ornaments, and to pack them away each year with the decorations, so you won't be embarrassed from one year to the next by not being able to remember who gave you the gilt cherub or the snowman with the light-up nose.) Fill in any bare spots on your tree with red and white checked bows that your party guests help you tie. As they work, you can set out a wassail bowl and bakery stollen instead of your usual party fare. If you can't fit in a tree-trimming party each year, you might simply make a habit of exchanging ornaments each Christmas with family members and close friends. Just start giving them to people, instead of or in addition to your other gifts, and they will quickly get into the spirit. My friend Jane Williams makes a point of annually giving an ornament to her goddaughter so she'll one day have a head start on creating a beautiful tree of her own —a lovely tradition you might share with your nieces and nephews. Instead of giving ornaments, I sometimes give friends the gift boxes of frankincense and myrrh that are available by mail from Aphrodisia (282 Bleecker Street, New York, New York 10014).

What you put under your tree can also go a long way toward brightening your home for the holidays. Wrap some of your gifts to others in computer print-out paper or in recent stock tables, depending on the interests of the recipient. Or wrap them in cut-up brown grocery bags jazzed up with shiny red notarial seals from a stationery or department store. Then keep all of your packages out under your tree for the entire season. One man who never got his shopping finished until December 24 nonetheless added a lot of holiday cheer to his place by wrapping up some huge empty boxes that he piled under a tall ponytail palm tree.

Even easier than putting up a tree is just hanging a stocking or putting out a festive centerpiece. Many craft or folk art stores sell stockings made from scraps of antique quilts, one of which hangs on my fireplace each Christmas. An easy and elegant holiday centerpiece consists simply of fresh cranberries piled in a clear glass or brass bowl, perhaps with some evergreen boughs arranged around it. A half dozen or so shiny red apples become an instant holiday decoration when you pile them in a basket around which you have tied a red and green checked ribbon. Try to display your Christmas cards in another ribbon-tied basket or arrayed traditionally on a mantelpiece.

A good way to decommercialize Christmas or Hanukkah is to make at least a few of your gifts to other people. Frame some photographs you've taken or cartoons you've clipped from magazines with special friends in mind. Or make food gifts for everybody: maybe chocolate truffles, brandied fruits, or small loaves of cranberry nut bread. You can generally find recipes for these and other edible presents in comprehensive cookbooks or in magazine holiday numbers. One of the easiest and most elegant food gifts you can make consists of about two dozen chocolate-dipped apricots. To make them, buy a box of dried apricots and a one-pound bar of semisweet chocolate. Melt the latter slowly in the top of a double boiler or in a small saucepan held over rapidly boiling water. Dip the apricots one at a time into the warm, melted chocolate, so that about one third of each is covered with a little chocolate cap. Allow them to dry on a cookie sheet or candy rack, and they are ready to wrap. These make especially nice host or hostess gifts for any dinner parties you're invited to during the season.

Another good way to involve yourself more fully in the holidays is to make your own cards or to send photo greeting cards, as I do each year. More single people than ever are realizing that the latter aren't just for families. In fact, photo cards have a particular benefit for men and women who aren't married. A lot of single people go for months or even years without getting a really good picture of themselves taken, because there often seems to be no one to take it. But just knowing that you're going to send out photo cards often keeps you on the lookout for people you can hand your camera over to on vacation to be sure that you get some good shots of yourself to use when the holidays roll around.

Finally, in the rush to buy and do things for other people,

don't forget to do a few for yourself. Treat yourself and a friend to a pair of tickets for *The Nutcracker* or Handel's "Messiah." (And don't forget that, if you want to get the best seats, you may have to order them in October or November.) Take in the annual Christmas tree lighting on your town green or go to midnight mass on December 24 at a neo-Gothic cathedral smelling of pine boughs and incense. And, if you dread the approach of yet another raucous and silly New Year's Eve, with or without a date, take a few moments to plan an elegant dinner party for six to twelve of your closest friends—the really *civilized* way to spend the last night of the year.

Most of all, carve out a little private time to reflect on the meaning of all the mad rushing about. A few well-chosen records on your stereo can do a lot to put you in the right frame of mind, especially if you curl up on the sofa to listen to them with a glass of hot mulled cider or wine in your hand. If you like classical music, put on some Renaissance carols or Bach's "Christmas Cantata." If your tastes run to more contemporary melodies, consider seasonal tunes played on the acoustic guitar by John Fahey, one of America's leading folk guitarists.

As the music fills your apartment, you might reread a favorite holiday story, whether it's Dickens' *A Christmas Carol* or Steinbeck's *The Red Pony*, and savor how lovely it is to have room in your life for such gentle pleasure. If or when you marry or have children, you'll still have the holidays. What you may not have is nearly so much peaceful time in which to contemplate just what, after all, the fuss is all about.

12

Getting Religion

In any Hall of Fame for Things Single People Usually Put Off Until They Get Married, attending religious services would rank right up there with wearing sensible pajamas and voting in school board elections. Like virginity, faith is something you were supposed to lose in college. Unlike virginity, faith is something you are supposed to get back, usually after you marry and have children.

Not that single people haven't had some good reasons for giving houses of worship the cold shoulder. Churches and synagogues traditionally have revolved around such events as Family Night suppers, Couples Club meetings, and Sunday School outings. What single man or woman could help but feel left out by them?

More recently, though, the major faiths have begun to seek out single people as never before and to try to make them feel welcome. Many churches hold retreats just for the unmarried or the divorced, and some temples have dances for young, single Jews. And any number of congregations have replaced their Couples Clubs with more inclusive Young Adult Clubs. The result is that many single men and women are reclaiming their religious heritage, with benefits that aren't just spiritual.

Among those benefits can be a fixed reference point in a life that may have few others. All too many single people find themselves to be constantly switching jobs, addresses, or romantic partners, to a point that nothing' seems the same from one day to the next. And, when that's true, a church or synagogue can become a badly needed still point in your day-to-day existence. Like a loving spouse, a house of worship can be something you can turn to for comfort and support from one season to the next. Its members can even come to comprise a sort of surrogate family that includes all ages, races, and nationalities, with whom you share valued rituals and traditions. As a young, single woman living in Manhattan, I loved attending services at Park Avenue United Methodist Church, not just for its excellent sermons, but also because it sponsored several Vietnamese refugee families it was a joy to get to know. Especially when you are in your twenties, your social life is likely to consist almost exclusively of other single people in your own age range. Through a congregation you can connect easily with people who *aren't* like you, which can be frankly refreshing.

Apart from giving you a ready-made family, participating in the affairs of a congregation can make you feel like a certified adult. It's nice to have a channel for your highest impulses, or a vehicle for social and community service. It almost can't be said too often: the most important way to be happily single isn't to see how much you can get from life but to see how much you can give to it. And one of your most urgent challenges is finding an outlet that allows you to contribute as much as you can as often as you can. Houses of worship, for all their flaws, give you that outlet. Whether by allowing you to help raise money for a new parsonage roof or to work for a few hours a week in a soup kitchen for the hungry, a church or synagogue lets you help other people, something that helps you to look beyond your own concerns.

But what you can get from belonging to a particular congregation is almost never as great as what you can get from faith itself. And, though some sort of stabilizing belief system is important for almost everybody, it can have particular value for people who are single.

For many people, marriage represents, in effect, a pseudoreligion. One member of a couple often finds in his or her spouse what some people discover in God: someone to look to for aid and comfort; someone to praise and adore; someone with whom to have an intimate relationship; and, above all, someone who makes life worth it. In fact, any number of married people seem almost literally to worship their spouses. Almost everybody knows at least one married man or woman who quotes his or her partner's breakfast conversation so solemnly that you'd think he or she had encountered Jeremiah over the Pop-Tarts. A single person without faith lacks not just a religion but the one thing that often serves as a substitute for it: marriage.

Whether you are single or married, faith gives you hope. At least it keeps you emotionally off the ropes. After surviving two life-threatening illnesses, editor Norman Cousins told a reporter: "Faith has a very important part in the healing process. Faith means the ability to breathe and have confidence, even when the evidence seems to point the other way." The Rev. Carl Scovel, of Boston's King's Chapel, has said: "Faith is the belief that, in spite of all outward appearances to the contrary, all will be well." Faith can help to heal a broken heart or the disappointment that results from not getting a promotion, and steady you when a lot of emotional ground seems to be shifting under your feet.

In many ways, it can be harder to be single today than in simpler times, when men and women commonly chalked their singlehood up to "the will of God" and then got on with living. Being single in a secular age can mean living without the consoling certainty that Somebody up There wants you to be single and thus without the knowledge that your marital status is both necessary and blessed.

Over and over again, I have heard single people say that they want to marry and have children and that they need to "do something" before it is too late. There is often a terrible and terrifying urgency in their voices, as though they alone bore total responsibility for their singlehood, for which they will one day be called to account.

Too few single people acknowledge the very real existence of forces beyond their control that come to bear on their marital status as surely as on anything else. Call it luck, chance, destiny, or God; whatever you label it, something in the world exists that you have no control over, and it is a shame to deny it.

Not to believe in something you can't control means that, for as long as you are single, you can never rest for a moment in the search for a partner, because the instant you chose to do so might be the one during which someone would have appeared, if only you had taken the time to blow-dry your hair or attend a party across town. To live without faith in what the philosopher William James called "something more" is to live with a perpetual legacy of self-blame for your singlehood because—just as there appears to be nothing but your own efforts to keep you from finding a spouse—neither is there anything to help you find one when the time is right. Not to believe in a force greater than your own will is to be, finally, alone, against all the odds.

But what if, quite simply, you've lost faith *in* faith? Or what if you were raised in a religion that now seems to fit you no better than a pair of childhood overalls?

In either case, the best way to reclaim some religious feeling isn't to rush back to the faith in which you were raised and which you may have long since outgrown. There is nothing to be gained by berating yourself for not being able to believe what you are supposed to. Try instead to figure out what you really *do* believe in and why.

Lodged deep inside you, there probably exists a strong feeling about whatever or whoever it was that kept you from getting killed in a freak bike accident when you were ten, that got you rejected by Williams but into Yale in a walk, or that kept you from marrying your college sweetheart who later turned out to be a borderline schizophrenic. Everybody holds something sacred, or at least in awe.

So try to define what you have faith in besides your own abilities. One useful tool is *The Road Less Traveled: Love, Traditional Values and a New Psychology of Spiritual Growth* (Simon & Schuster, 1978), by M. Scott Peck, which looks at human spiritual needs in light of contemporary psychological perspectives. The bestselling *When Bad Things Happen to Good People* (Avon, 1983), by Rabbi Harold S. Kushner, takes a fresh look at an old question: if God exists, why are there such things as heart disease, plane crashes, and the loss of people you love?

Don't hesitate, in your spiritual odyssey, to poke around in different faiths, denominations, or houses of worship. It's fun and enlightening to try on different systems of belief, and you may find one that suits you far better than the one you grew up with. Inside the lukewarm Methodist that you have always been there may be a red-hot Episcopalian dying to get out. A lapsed Reform Jew might find his or her true religious identity in a Reconstructionist *havurah*, where the emphasis is on reclaiming culture and tradition while avoiding stuffiness and rigidity.

As a single man or woman, you are likely to have unprecedented opportunities to soak up other religions while attending religious services with friends or dates, who can help you understand what they are all about. As someone else's guest, I have visited a Quaker meeting, a Passover seder, a Shrove Tuesday pancake breakfast, and a Buddhist zendo ringing with the chants of *nam myoho renge kyo*. You might attend a bat mitzvah or a 1980s version of the 1970s folk mass, with electric guitars. If you are feeling somehow spiritually at sea, try to attend as many different sorts of services as you can and to talk to people about them. Not the least of the advantages of doing that when you are single is that you can do so without running your actions by your parents or a spouse, who might not share your enthusiasms.

A lot of single people say: "But how can I go to church if I don't have any faith?" The question might be turned around to read: "How can you have faith if you don't go to church?" Wanting to have a better relationship with God when you never enter a house of worship is like wanting to have a better relationship with a relative whom you never go to visit.

Some single people say: "But how can I attend a church or synagogue if I don't believe everything it teaches?" The answer is that nobody is asking you to believe everything it teaches. Just go for whatever you enjoy and feel comfortable appreciating: the music, the friendliness of the other parishioners, or the restful pause in the week's activity. You probably don't support every position taken by the company for which you work, but you don't quit your job because of it. So why should houses of worship be exempt from the same sort of benefit of the doubt that you give to your employer and others?

It's also important to note that you may be surprised by what you discover when you attend services even in a denomination that you think you know well. A lot of separated and divorced Catholics, for instance, dropped out of churches in an era when the formerly married often felt ostracized by them. Today, it's a rare urban church that doesn't have programs aimed at making them feel at home. The North American Conference of Separated and Divorced Catholics is working to bring about other changes that would make them feel still more at ease.

Finding a church or synagogue that you'll want to play an active role in may not be easy. Some houses of worship still *do* make single people feel like odd men and women out. But fewer and fewer of them each year take that stance.

And more of them reflect the spirit of a Presbyterian minister in Pittsburgh who not long ago preached a sermon entitled, "Jesus Was a Bachelor, Too." If you are young and having trouble finding a church or temple with a lot of people in your own age group, visit one on or near a college campus. If you are Jewish and can't afford to get tickets to High Holy Days services at a nearby synagogue, call the Hillel office of a nearby university, which can probably tell you where to attend a service for free, or where to find an open seder if you can't go home for Passover.

Most of all, don't give up. Somewhere there is a religion, a denomination, or a spiritual group in which you can feel at home. And one key to finding it is to remember that the purpose of spiritual exploration isn't to give you the answers to all your metaphysical questions. It's to give you ways of looking at—and making sense of—complex issues that will never be resolved once and for all.

Wherever your spiritual journey ultimately takes you, a comforting knowledge will usually result. In the eyes of God, fate, destiny, or anything else you call it, everybody stands alone. So, by finding your faith, you are also discovering the one place in your life where your marital status can and does make no difference at all.

13

The (New) Case for Marrying Later

For most of this book, I've been urging you to stop fixating on marriage and start appreciating what you have now. But does that mean you should never wed at all? Of course not!

For most people the question isn't whether to marry or to remarry but when. More than ninety percent of all Americans will wed before they die, and more than three quarters of the divorced will tie the knot again. Most people also know, practically from birth, that they *want* to marry. So the real issue isn't whether to stay single for a lifetime. It is when to exchange the freedoms and restrictions of singlehood for the freedoms and restrictions of matrimony. Even if you love being single you may find yourself asking: How much of a good thing is too much of one? If I wait to wed, won't I eventually lose more than I gain?

A generation ago, the answers were clear-cut. Singlehood provided virtually the only route by which many people could escape the then stifling restrictions on married couples. Having no children or only one, common practice today, was almost unheard of. Tying the knot meant locking yourself not just into a marriage but inevitably into parent-hood and a lifetime of multiple responsibilities.

Because children had to be educated, and because most couples lacked the second income that made private schools more affordable, getting married also meant moving to suburbia where the public ones were good. And nobody needs much reminding that women were expected to give up their careers and find fulfillment, as Erma Bombeck once put it, "by cleaning chrome faucets with a toothbrush." To wed a generation ago was, quite literally, to turn your life inside out.

Today, couples are freer than ever to custom-design a partnership according to their own needs. They can even choose to live essentially as they did when single. So why would anybody want to go it alone for a while when marriage has come to offer more flexibility than ever?

Perhaps the most obvious answer is that people still treat you differently when you are part of a couple. In marriage you aren't just seen as yourself but as an extension of your spouse. The two of you are expected to go places and to do things together or simply to "settle down."

Even couples who've lived together before their wedding may find themselves confronted by new obligations. A *New Yorker* cartoon once showed two men discussing the changes that marriage brings about. "Well, yes," one is saying. "There *is* a difference. When you're just living together, you don't have to buy the French copper pots at forty bucks a throw." A lot of married people manage to resist the unrelenting pressure to act like a couple. The pressure, however, is still there—and may not be welcome when you face all too much already.

Then again, even if you want someday to wed, marriage may not be your highest priority. This tends especially to be true for people whose devotion to a career approaches the level of a calling. The higher your aspirations, the harder it can be to fulfill them along with marital obligations. Contrary to a lot of what you read in the media today, not everybody can or should "have it all." It can be downright exhausting to be a twenty-four-hour-a-day Super Mom or Super Dad, and sometimes it is smart not even to try.

At best, trying to reach the heights when you are married can be a little like trying to scale a mountain with an extra pack strapped to your back—an idea well expressed in some of Rudyard Kipling's most famous lines:

> Down to Gehenna
> Or up to the throne
> He travels fastest
> Who travels alone.

Gail Sheehy made a similar point in *Pathfinders* (Morrow, 1981), a study of contemporary trailblazers. She wrote: "Achieving *excellence* in some endeavor requires ignoring balance during at least one phase of life. For a person who is graced with uncommon athletic ability or artistic talent, or with obvious nurturant gifts or pure brain power, and who wishes to develop that endowment to the limit, a fierce and singular focus is generally demanded in the early years of adulthood." Finding that focus can mean, quite literally, remaining single.

Going it alone can have particular value for people who are in the most formative years of their careers. That, at least, was a conclusion drawn by Mary Alice Kellogg, following a survey of the nation's young superachievers whom she described in *Fast Track* (McGraw-Hill, 1978). "Those who have made it to the top young these days are likely to be loners, pure and simple," she wrote. But Kellogg added that the term "loner" need not be a put-down. It can also refer to someone "with friends and all the positive societal trappings, someone who is simply different in a private way."

More than ever, the pages of Who's Who turn up the names of unmarried superstars who are "different" by virtue of their singleness. They include politicians Ed Koch and Jerry Brown, anchorwoman Diane Sawyer, athletes Carl and Carol Lewis, activists Gloria Steinem and Ralph

Nader, and singer Linda Ronstadt. All hit it big in their thirties or younger, suggesting that the lack of a spouse not only didn't hold them back but helped them reach the top. Countless others have waited to marry until safely enthroned upon the heights, including actress Sally Field, anchorwoman Connie Chung, singers Bruce Springsteen and Olivia Newton-John, agent Irving ("Swifty") Lazar, and "Today Show" host Jane Pauley and her husband, cartoonist Garry Trudeau.

It seems that, by freeing you from many of the day-to-day demands of domesticity, singlehood allows you to respond to the world at large instead of to the one tugging at your apron strings. And this tends especially to be true for the writers, artists, and others whose works require isolation. The history books are filled with the names of unmarried men and women who made a creative difference: Marcel Proust, Henry James, Emily Dickinson, Franz Schubert, Vincent Van Gogh, Leonardo da Vinci, Jane Austen, and Ludwig van Beethoven.

It's not hard to see, though, why singlehood particularly benefits Yuppies. The older you get, the better equipped you become to juggle conflicting priorities. It thus becomes that much easier to accommodate both marriage and a career and to do well at each.

A later marriage can be less a luxury than a necessity for someone who had a less-than-enchanted childhood. A serene and happy youth tends to leave you sweet and trusting and able to love and be loved easily. A more complicated childhood often makes it harder for you to grow close to people when you are older. At least, it can require that you spend more time learning to achieve intimacy in singlehood before you try to reach it with a spouse.

The kind of marriage your parents had exerts a particularly powerful influence on your ability to form close ties to others and therefore on how long you may want or need to wait to wed. If your parents weren't Ward and June Cleaver —or if you grew up in what was frankly a battle zone—

singlehood can become a sort of DMZ that lets you gather strength while enjoying some badly needed peace and tranquillity. There is no point rushing into a marriage that might subject you all too soon to some of the same sorts of stresses you faced while growing up.

Even single people who came from happy families may fear that they will grow too rigid or set in their ways to make a good marriage. That rarely seems to happen. In fact, at least one survey found that the odds for finding happiness in marriage increase with every year you wait to wed, up to age twenty-five.

Later marriages may be better partly because the people who enter them are more mature. If age were the only factor that mattered, however, second marriages ought to have a far lower divorce rate than first ones, because the people who make them are older than people tying the knot for the first time.

Second marriages, in reality, have a slightly *higher* divorce rate than first ones. A possible explanation is that most people remarry within three years of getting their final decree, or having spent little time on their own. The critical variable may well be, not how old you are when you marry or remarry, but how much time you have spent doing a solo run. The better you know yourself, it seems, the better your chances for picking the right sort of partner for you.

After you have dried behind the ears, you can forge a different kind of marriage than you could have when younger. Later marriages, for instance, are less likely to have a breadwinner and a bread baker. Most women who've been single have learned how to support themselves, and most men who've lived alone have mastered some of the finer points of cooking and cleaning. So their marriages are likely to be freer of sex-role expectations. Two people who wait until their late twenties or older to wed are also far less apt to find that their expectations of each other change dramatically in midstream, a common cause of divorce.

But will they still be able to have children? It's true that the risk of birth defects increases with the age of both parents and not just, as is commonly believed, with the age of the mother. As Wenda Wardell Morrone reports in *Pregnant While You Work* (Macmillan, 1984), a *man's* age becomes a possible risk at forty-one and a probable risk at fifty-five.

Yet, just as awareness of the risks of later parenthood has increased, so have the techniques that can help to minimize them. Couples having their first child this year can benefit from amniocentesis, fetal heart monitors, and even in-utero surgery, all of them unknown until not too long ago. The men and women still deferring parenthood may find, by the time they are ready to embark on it, that they can avail themselves of other medical breakthroughs that can't now be imagined.

A lot of people worry that, even if they are able to have children at a later age, they will have less energy for them. A thirty-three-year-old divorced man expressed the fears of many of his peers when he admitted to me: "I don't want to be a grandfather to my children."

But such fears, too, can turn out to be baseless. At least one cliché about parenthood really does have a basis in fact: children "keep you young." No matter when they arrive, they give you a second wind. I once wrote an article on later motherhood for *Parents* magazine, for which I interviewed dozens of people who'd had a first child at thirty or thirty-five. Expecting to hear the pros and cons of later parenthood in equal measure, I was startled to discover that no couples wished they had started a family earlier. The people I interviewed insisted that they didn't believe they had less energy for their children than they would have had when younger. Many said they used to feel that they had to pour an enormous amount of themselves into their career. Now that they are older, they aren't so driven to give so much at the office; instead they can divert some of their energy from their work to their children.

Perhaps more significantly, many older parents have long since made regular exercise a part of their lives. They are much fitter than they were as teenagers or in their early twenties, or even in better shape than some of their younger friends.

Older parents, finally, tend to have more money and are better able to hire household help. They don't need to run themselves ragged retrieving Big Bird puppets from under the coffee table, because a housekeeper or baby-sitter can do a lot of chores for them.

It would be a mistake, even so, to suggest that the benefits of remaining single consist mostly of what it can do for an eventual marriage. The truth is that you may *not* wed, nor may you reach a level in your profession that allows you retroactively to justify staying single for it. And, apart from anything it can do someday for something or somebody else, time to yourself can do a lot for you right now.

One thing singlehood can do is simply give you a little license to experiment with different styles of being. After years of having to answer to your parents or a spouse, you can be your own boss, which can seem an overwhelming relief. On a whim, you can change your name, your occupation, your hairstyle, or your lifestyle, all without having to explain your actions to someone else.

Accountable only to yourself, you also have more leeway with your time and your money than you would be likely to have in a marriage. That means you may be able to explore interests you won't have a chance to pursue again. You can spend your last dime on a trip to Cancun, on an antique piano, on a postdoctoral study program, or on a bouquet of the first jonquils of spring, to see how much one of them does for you. As a single adult, I've certainly made mistakes: gone out with the wrong man, taken a dead-end job, or failed to give a friendship its due. But none of those errors was one that I couldn't recover from or learn from before it was too late.

Learning from your mistakes obviously matters in marriage, too. But it can be harder to do, because it is less easy to say which were yours and which were someone else's. A spouse might also find it harder to forgive you for things for which you can easily forgive yourself. One result is that being single often lets you remain on a steeper part of a learning curve than marriage could or would, because you are less likely to take someone with you should you fall off.

Nice as it might be to have someone around when you want to hang a picture or hear noises on the fire escape, the day-to-day demands of marriage exact a price all their own. Married life especially reduces your privacy, which can cut into your creativity. Too many single people forget, as a celebrated architecture professor once noted, that privacy is "one of the last luxuries left." It can also be a necessity for people in the arts and related fields or for people who simply have interests that require a measure of solitude. Had I married in my early twenties, I might never have faced a dateless Saturday night or a vacation alone. But I also might not have written one book, edited two others, and contributed to several more. I also might not have been able to take three all-expense-paid business trips to Europe . . . or appear on talk shows throughout the country . . . or fly off at a moment's notice to interview celebrities like Chris Evert, Kurt Vonnegut, and Marlo Thomas. Having a spouse, it seems, is a little like going through life with background music always playing. You may *like* it, but you also always *hear* it, and it can distract you, even if it at other times soothes.

But isn't there a chance that if you wait to wed—and especially if you wait without spending a lot of time looking for a partner—you may never marry at all? Of course. But there are no guarantees that you will marry even if you spend every waking moment lining up dates.

Besides, most people have an inner timer that tells them when they are ready to marry. And yours may simply not have sounded yet, or what you have heard may be a false alarm. The columnist Ellen Goodman once wondered whether a marriage-minded single friend was "merely appeasing the gods of her upbringing by assuring them that she, too, wants what she was taught to want." A lot of other single adults are trying to placate the same deities. Many have lived for so long with the idea that they will or should wed that they often don't recognize that they really don't *want* to be married.

Enjoying what you have now often requires putting aside the belief that marriage is supposed to happen at certain times or in certain ways. When you are single in your late twenties or early thirties, it's easy to begin pushing panic buttons right and left. You may start to worry that you are falling so far behind that you can never "catch up" with your friends who already own wedding rings or baby strollers. But there's no statute of limitations on marriage. Because good partnerships always involve more than a little luck, you can never tell how things will work out, for you or for the friends who now inspire such mortal envy. You may be able to make a better marriage at thirty-five than someone else made at twenty-five—or than *you* could have made at twenty-five. You may also change your mind about the number of children you do or don't want, especially if you someday acquire a station wagonful of stepchildren.

Getting the most from the present inevitably requires that you stop trying to rewrite your past, even as you attempt to predict your own future. Yes, your life might have been different if you'd married that dashing premed major who pursued you throughout your senior year in college. But you didn't and have nothing to gain by beating up on yourself for it. Your life might also change radically if you were to meet your future spouse tomorrow. But there is still a lot of happiness to be uncovered in what you have today: good friends, books, music, art, and pathways to explore in the woods in the spring. Mozart is never less than Mozart because you listen to him alone, and the pleasures of making a perfectly risen raspberry soufflé aren't diminished because you prepare it for a friend instead of a mate.

As the divorce rate has increased, many people have asserted that something is "wrong" with marriage. But nothing may be wrong with marriage except that people still enter into it too soon. It is simply myth that today's men and women are staying single longer than those of any previous generation and that their decision to remain unwed is somehow fraying the fabric of family life.

In 1890, the first year for which the national census figures were kept, the median age at first marriage was 26.1 years for men and 22.0 years for women. In 1982, the median age at first marriage was 25.2 years for men, or lower than it was at the turn of the century. Also in 1982, it was 22.5 years for women, or only slightly higher than it was a hundred years ago. So why all the fuss in the media about how people are staying single so much longer? Because, quite simply, they are staying single longer than their *parents*, who married younger than any group in history! As one demographer put it: "What is remarkable is not that the Baby Boomers are marrying too late but that their parents married so early." But many of their elders were reacting to the disruptions in their lives caused by World War II, an excuse the current generation doesn't have.

The statistics make clear that, back in the days of Great-Grandma and -Grandpa, people took their time about marrying. And that fact may go a long way toward explaining why Great-Grandma and -Grandpa tended to stick together. Each of them also faced a shorter life span than do their descendants. In the 1890s, people married in their twenties and could be expected to live until roughly age fifty. In the 1980s, people generally marry in their twenties and can expect to live into their seventies. Although the extended life span reflects a drop in infant mortality rates as much as years tacked onto old age, marriages are still expected to last about twenty-five percent longer than they did a hundred years ago. Margaret Mead apparently was right when she remarked that one reason marriage worked so well in the nineteenth century was that people only lived until age fifty.

No less than ever, people expect their marriages to last for a lifetime. Yet too many are unwilling to wait even as long as their grandparents did to select a partner. It would make more sense for single people to learn at least to take care of themselves before they try to take care of another or ask someone else to return the favor.

Learning to stand physically and emotionally on two feet can rarely be done quickly. But what it can lead to is an intoxicating sense of self-sufficiency and the knowledge that you can flourish, with marriage or without it. Mastering the challenges of singlehood allows you to marry not from weakness but from strength and not because you *need* to but because you *want* to. If or when you wed, marriage may be the frosting on the cake but it will never be the whole cake.

You never know, finally, how you will feel about your marital status in a few years. Like a taste for caviar or white truffles, a taste for being single is often an acquired one. Some people pick it up in childhood and others don't acquire it until late middle age. Quite simply, one of the things nobody ever tells you about life on your own is how much your attitudes toward it can change. Not being married at twenty-one isn't the same as not being married at thirty-one or even at forty-one. And, while the usual assumption is that things get worse, they instead tend to get better, at least until you hit old age, and then they get worse for everybody, married or not. Once you have acquired a gray hair or two, you are smarter, more self-confident, more financially secure, and more at peace with the world than you were in your youth. Life is better simply because *you* are—and that can make being single a lot better, too.

Not everybody ultimately will agree with Henry David Thoreau, who wrote:

"I find it wholesome to be alone the greatest part of the time. To be in company, even with the best, is soon wearisome and dissipating. I love to be alone. I never found a companion that was so companionable as solitude."

But almost everybody can profit from getting to know him or herself before getting to know a spouse. Being single has always been more complex and challenging than the stereotypes suggest. And that is only one reason why—no less than being married—it can give you time to live, to learn, to love, and, above all, as the poet May Sarton has written, "time to *be*."

14

The Art of Being Single, or How to Pass for a Grown-up

> *"Freedom is like taking a bath; you've got to keep doing it every day."*
>
> Flo Kennedy

Contrary to popular belief, marriage does not automatically endow you with unlimited quantities of peace, happiness, and Le Creuset cookware, all of which are among the fringe benefits the institution is reputed to offer. There is, however, one thing that marriage does confer on almost everyone, and that is a sense that real life has begun. Marriage, inevitably, makes you feel like a grown-up.

Even couples who've lived together for years report that subtle changes occur once they make their partnership legal. Suddenly, they take themselves more seriously. They begin to speak in grave tones about things like life insurance, estate taxes, and little-known hereditary diseases. They argue about whether it is a federal offense to feed a child SpaghettiOs and, if so, whether the crime is a felony or simply a misdemeanor.

After you have married, other people tend to take you more seriously, too. Friends and coworkers congratulate you. Other married couples praise your good judgment. Even your partner's relatives, who barely spoke to you before, may begin to send you flowery birthday cards and demand to sit next to you at Aunt Ethel's seder. To all, you're a convert to the International Brotherhood of Adults.

Marriage, of course, doesn't confer maturity any more than a trip to Paris confers the ability to speak French. Nonetheless, marriage often forces you to learn new behavior patterns, just as a trip to Paris may force you to learn the French for "Excuse me, sir, but your Citroën is parked on my foot." Necessity reveals the depth and breadth of human potential. Marriage, in other words, often shames you into growing up.

As a single man or woman, you have nobody to shame you into anything, so you are free to live, not just in a state of suspended animation, but in suspended adolescence, rebelling less against your parents than against your own emerging adulthood. A lot of single people keep living this way for years, less because they want to than because they don't know another way. As the psychoanalyst Natalie Shainess observes in *Sweet Suffering* (Bobbs-Merrill, 1984), people behave self-destructively not because they enjoy feeling pain but because they don't know how not to. The trick is to remember that you don't have to be able to change your whole life in order to be able to do a few things that eventually will begin to add up.

Here, then, are some final things you can do right now to stop waiting for marriage or remarriage and start living.

Tame Your Time

The two great freedoms of singlehood are the freedom to spend your time and the freedom to spend your money without having to account for either to somebody else. But if I had to choose the greater of the two, I would choose the first, because it is in the use of their time that single people gain their biggest advantage over married ones. A lot of married people, particularly two-income couples, have more money at their disposal than do their single counterparts. But not many have more time, and most have less, because they have to invest a great deal of it in the marriage itself.

A single person's use of time therefore becomes a sort of existential trump card that can offset what might otherwise be the disadvantages of not having a spouse. An unattached man or woman needn't have a social life less exciting than that of a couple when he or she is willing to devote more time to creating one. Neither does a single person need to have a less successful career when he or she can devote more hours to a special project at work.

The trick to using your time effectively is to set goals before it's too late. Some things you can only do now—and others will be there for you for years. So try to understand the difference and act on it every day.

It's especially important to set goals besides the professional ones you will likely achieve anyway. You've usually got to work hard just to hold onto your job. But it's no less risky to pin most of your hopes on your career than to pin all of them on marriage. As former Senator Paul Tsongas noted, in *Heading Home* (Knopf, 1984), quoting a friend: "No one on his death bed ever said: 'I wish I had spent more time on my business.'"

One easy way to begin to get a handle on goals of many sorts is to read a good book on time management. I couldn't have pulled my own single years together without the aid of Alan Lakein's *How to Get Control of Your Time and Your Life* (Signet, 1974), which I try to reread at least once a year.

Whatever your goals, it's essential to write them down. Don't just keep a daily to-do list of things to be accomplished each day. Keep master lists of books you want to read, of dishes you want to cook, and of places you want to visit. Make a little game of crossing each one off as you accomplish it. One way to combine both daily and master lists is to invest in an 8 1/2 × 11-inch spiral notebook of the sort you used in school. Keep your daily to-do lists in this notebook, assigning a page to each day. But don't rip the page out after each night; keep it in place for future reference. This will quickly give you a fix on what sort of important goals continually keep getting brushed aside. I use the right side of the page, in my own spiral notebook, for my daily to-do lists; the left side I use for master lists of big goals in different categories. Once a month or so I flip through the notebook to see which goals I'm staying on top of and which ones are getting lost.

Jot your most important goals down on index cards and put them up where you can see them. A lot of newspaper readers were astonished to learn that the legendary Carl Yastrzemski, in his twenty-third and last season as a professional ballplayer, still wrote himself little notes on how to swing his bat. These he taped to the door of his clubhouse locker so he wouldn't miss them before a game. After an article describing his note writing came out, Yaz admitted in an interview that he couldn't understand the fuss about it. After all, he said, he'd been putting up such notes throughout his entire professional career.

More than two decades after selling my first article to a newspaper, I still tack up quotations to remind me how to write better. One of my favorites, which has hung above my typewriter for almost a decade, comes from the music critic Ernest Newman:

"The greatest composer does not sit down to work because he is inspired, but becomes inspired because he is working. Beethoven, Wagner, Bach, and Mozart settled down day after day to the job in hand with as much regularity as an accountant settles down to his figures. They didn't waste time waiting for inspiration."

So, too, it is with the greatest writers—and with the people who get the most out of life itself. The people who most enjoy living don't waste time waiting to be struck by lightning bolts of happiness that may never arrive. Their happiness is not contingent on their finding work, love, more money, or a bigger apartment. They simply settle down to enjoying each day as it comes and finding whatever joy there is to be had in the moment at hand.

Find an Existential Mentor

Almost nothing helps you focus your goals so much as knowing someone who's already achieved some with a grace you admire. Curiously, however, you don't always need to discuss your aims with that someone to profit from his or her example. You just need to be close enough to your role model to study how he or she responds in situations you're likely to encounter.

It helps if your existential mentor is someone you perceive to be older and wiser, but age and experience matter less than such things as personal integrity and judgment. My own mentors have included a former college professor along with at least one or two people quite close to my own age.

One woman I know describes her relations with her personal mentor this way:

"I love my parents dearly and never hesitated to look to them for advice when I was growing up. But now I can't always expect them to give me what I need, because they see me as the girl I was instead of as the woman I'm trying to become. So I now use as my role model someone I met at church and whom I see there often as we work on various projects. I don't always consult her when a problem presents itself, because I can often solve it on my own. But I do always try to think about how she would handle it—what questions she would ask herself and how she would proceed. This seems to help to keep me on the sort of path I want to be on, by making sure that I respond as a person I admire might."

Pick a Paper Mentor, Too

Apart from your personal mentor, you can benefit by having what I call a "paper mentor," an author who can inspire you when the people you need aren't around. I'm not talking about a fiction writer into whose words you can escape (though I hope you'll come to know more than one of those, too). I'm talking about someone who has written extensively about his or her own life, particularly at the age you are now, and from whose example you can profit. The kind of author you need to know is someone who always seems to explain you to yourself, offering thoughts you didn't know you had until you saw them on the printed page.

I found my first paper mentor, while still a college student, when I came across the letters and diaries of Anne Morrow Lindbergh. Lindbergh's papers begin in her childhood and continue through early middle age. So I often was able to watch her mature, through her own diaries and letters, even as I was trying to do the same.

A bit later, I moved on to the essays of E. B. White, whose *Elements of Style* had steered me through years of college writing assignments. Scarcely a week passes that I do not dip, however briefly, into one of White's wise and compassionate works. The author writes about nature with an almost pantheistic reverence, so that I can scarcely open one of his books without feeling more kindly disposed toward all creation. Why not find someone who'll have the same effect on you?

It's also important to keep reading the life histories of people you admire, even though they may have been written by someone else. These are essentially your textbooks for adult life—the places you can turn to in order to find out how other people got through what you're going through. I have found few better cures for bouts of loneliness or depression than plunking myself down in the biography section of a local bookstore or library, then browsing among the shelves until I find a life that inspires me to move forward.

Reading fiction is important, too, because it teaches you things you can't learn any other way. To grow you've often got to watch other people respond over time so that you can benefit from their example. Novels help you do this by showing you character unfolding on their pages.

One single woman I know "adopts" one writer a year. Ellen devotes the year to reading as many works as she can of a particular author. She'll do Willa Cather one year, Henry James the next, and Eudora Welty after that. She reads all of the author's major novels or short stories and tries to get through his or her biography, too. (Ellen also occasionally picks up a copy of a Cliffs Note, just to make sure she's getting everything she could out of a book.) She sometimes also takes a course in her favorite author at a local night school. And all of this makes Ellen, not a hopeless literary drone, but one of the most sought-after guests on the cocktail party circuit in her town. People know her as someone who can always be counted on to refer a recent migrant workers' dispute back to the Joad family in *The Grapes of Wrath* or to inject a well-known quote from *My Ántonia* into a lively debate about the third wave of feminism. The last time one of her admirers got the flu, she sat at his bedside and read him short stories by John Cheever while spoon-feeding him cassis sherbet, neither of which hurt her cause in the least.

If you can't find time to finish a book, read newspapers and magazine articles likely to inspire you. In need of a quick fix of encouragement, I often turn to the daily editorial in the *Christian Science Monitor,* invariably an upbeat message on a topic such as hope, love, kindness, or resilience. This dauntless paper also publishes, every Tuesday, a column called "The Loose Leaf Notebook," comprising a brief work or excerpt from the writings of great authors from Homer to Hemingway, a good place to start picking up where your college lit classes left off.

Try especially to read something enriching before you go to sleep each night, to give yourself something to dream on. Keep a notebook or card file in which you jot down your favorite passages or quotations and new words you want to look up. My bedside table usually contains the likes of *The Collected Poems of Emily Dickinson*, the Episcopal *Book of Common Prayer*, one of the collections of E. B. White's essays mentioned earlier, and perhaps a Barbara Pym novel. If I were banished tomorrow to a desert island, I would take them all with me and count myself rich in company.

If you lack the time to read books, at least listen to them on tape. They can be bought at many large bookstores or be rented by mail from Books on Tape, Inc. (P. O. Box 7900, Newport Beach, California 92660). Books on Tape lets you maneuver in and out of the fast lane on the freeway while listening to any of hundreds of abridged or full-length fiction or nonfiction books, from classics such as *War and Peace* to recent bestsellers. I listen to Tolstoy on my Walkman, while waiting for planes or walking from one appointment to the next.

Hear the Music

As a superannuated child of the sixties, I would be the last person to suggest that you pack your *Abbey Road* albums off to the Salvation Army along with your back issues of *Rolling Stone.* Nobody, however, can live well by rock music alone.

Perhaps you already know that your heart belongs to Donizetti or Dvořák. If not, you might pick up a few of the tapes in the Columbia Stereo Cassette Series featuring the best-loved works of the major composers. These have such titles as *Beethoven's Greatest Hits* (#16 11 0106) or *Handel's Greatest Hits* (#16 11 0124). Time-Life recordings puts out a wonderful series of albums of the great composers' masterworks that includes a commentary on each. Why not study one composer a month for a year? Enhance your enjoyment by taking a music appreciation course at the local adult ed center or by reading Harold C. Schonberg's marvelous *The Lives of the Great Composers* (Norton, 1981), a collection of lively, lucid profiles of people whose music never goes out of fashion.

Without so much as taking a course or reading a book, you can expand your knowledge of their works by tuning in regularly to the best classical music station in your area. Keep a pad and pencil beside your stereo or radio to jot down the names of selections you've enjoyed and may want to buy. Many stations announce the manufacturer and catalogue number for each piece of music aired, which can help you to find your favorites in local stores. Possibly the best classical music program in America is Karl Haas's "Adventures in Good Music," syndicated to more than six hundred stations nationwide. Haas does for classical music what Julia Child did for French cooking, carving it up and serving it with such verve that it appeals even to people who thought they couldn't stand it. Don't miss the syndicated "Adventures" if it airs in your area.

Get Cultured

Like great books and music, great performances are Valium for the spirit. If I never enter another theater or concert hall, I will still die a happy woman for having seen Mikhail Baryshnikov and Gelsey Kirkland dance the *pas de deux* from *Don Quixote* and listened to the Boston Symphony Orchestra under the maples at Tanglewood. To reap similar rewards, you need to begin to get a handle on the many that may be offered in your area. Go through the entertainment section of the Sunday paper each week and clip out ads for events that might interest you. Call or write as soon as you can for tickets to those you're sure you'll want to attend. Clip the ads for others to your desk calendar at the office, on the days they'll take place. That way, if you decide you want to attend a lecture or concert at the last minute, you'll have all the details in front of you, not buried in a stack of papers at home.

I used to try to attend one major performance in every major art form each year: one opera, one ballet, one classical music concert, one major art exhibit, and so forth. This method provides a good way to insure that you'll get at least a subsistence diet of culture when it's too expensive to go to a feast. Once you develop a feel for the art forms you like best, you might buy season tickets in a double subscription. That way you'll begin to experience some in more depth, especially if you offer your extra ticket to a friend more knowledgable about the form than you are.

Another way to begin to get a handle on the cultural offerings in your city is to have a specialty. My friend Barbara is a Gilbert and Sullivan fan who can always ferret out a fellow Savoyard with whom to enjoy a performance of *Iolanthe* or *The Pirates of Penzance*. Jeff, a newspaper editor, prefers the salsa music of his beloved San Antonio. My specialty is Shakespearean drama, chosen because I never studied the Bard in college and have struggled ever since to tell Prospero from Pericles. I feed my habit by attending theatrical productions mounted by local colleges, straw-hat theaters, and professional repertory companies, and by trying to take in Shakespeare plays in the movies, on TV, and in other media. I hit the jackpot the year I saw James Earl Jones in the Broadway show *Othello* only a few weeks before I caught Shirley Verrett as Desdemona in Verdi's *Otello*, staged by the Opera Company of Boston. One of these days I may decide I didn't need that Intro to Elizabethan Theater course after all, but in the meantime I'm learning a lot that I couldn't get in a classroom.

Have Children in Your Life

Just because you're single doesn't mean you can't have children around you. Friends will often be only too happy to let you borrow their offspring for a day trip to the zoo or for an evening of making popcorn and watching *Mary Poppins* or *Star Wars* on your VCR.

Better still, establish a continuing relationship with a child who needs you. Join the Big Brother or Big Sister organization or the Jewish Big Brother or Big Sister program. Lead a Scout troop, coach in a Saturday morning soccer league, or do volunteer work at an orphanage or foundling hospital.

Even if you lack time for regular activities you can support and write to a child through an overseas sponsorship program. Two of the most respected are Save the Children (54 Wilton Road, Westport, Connecticut 06880) and the Foster Parents Plan (1555 Plan Way, Warwick, Rhode Island 02887). Either allows you to sponsor a child for under twenty-five dollars a month. More than fifty years old, Save the Children has flourished owing partly to its continuing support from the British Royal Family. The Foster Parents Plan, founded in 1937, places special emphasis on developing a strong sponsor-child relationship. Letters between the two are particularly encouraged. Foster Parents are also permitted to visit "their" children overseas or on Indian reservations in the United States. Through sponsorship of a ten-year-old Ecuadoran girl I've been able to attend regular get-togethers of Foster Parents in my city, arranged by Plan staff members, and have never talked with anyone who found the experience less enriching than I do.

Especially as you move into your thirties and beyond, children do as much for you as you do for them. In a widely quoted speech urging citizens of the British Commonwealth to learn from its youngest subjects, Queen Elizabeth II said: "We could use some of that sturdy confidence, that

devastating honesty with which children rescue us from
self-doubts and self-delusion. . . . Above all, we must retain the child's readiness to forgive with which we are all
born and which it is all too easy to lose as we grow older." In
the absence of the next generation it is all too easy to forget
life isn't about being able to afford the latest model car or
Cuisinart—it's about sharing what you've learned with others so their lives will be a little easier.

Champion a Cause

One of the most wonderful things about being single is
that you have the time to give to your community and the
many organizations that comprise it. You don't have to
stand passively by when you hear that a hundred-year-old
Beaux Arts theater may be torn down to make way for yet
another fast food palace; you can draw up a petition, collect
signatures, go to City Council meetings, and make a real
difference in the way things turn out. You can speak out,
sometimes because you needn't worry that any controver-
sial positions you take will adversely affect your family.

How do you find the organization that needs you the
most? Mostly, you read newspapers, talk to your friends,
and send away for information. Then you join the groups
that need you the most. It's almost impossible to list all of
the possible categories of organizations that would love to
have your help. There are environmental groups (Green-
peace, the Sierra Club, or the National Wildlife Federation),
religious groups (B'nai B'rith, Church Women United, the
National Conference of Separated and Divorced Catholics),
and men's or women's groups (NOW, Fathers United for
Equal Justice, and Mothers Without Custody). And nobody
can't find at least one organization that badly needs his or
her support. I am partial to Oxfam America, dedicated to
relieving world hunger and related problems; to the Red
Cross, a provider of disaster relief at everything from earth-
quake sites to marathon finish lines; and to the American

Civil Liberties Union, which takes on unpopular causes so that the rest of us can live and speak more freely. In my own city, I support the Beacon Hill Civic Association, the Massachusetts Cultural Alliance, and many other groups. It doesn't matter whether you donate your time and money to a strictly local group or to a worldwide one. What matters is that you find one that lets you contribute the best that's in you to give. Somewhere in the world, there exists a truly terrific, selfless life-affirming organization that needs your help. And one of the nicest things you can do for yourself and for it is to find that group and support it with your time, your energy, and your money. If you would like to do volunteer work for a needy group but aren't sure which one could use your help, call the United Way and ask for the location of its nearest Voluntary Action Centers, a clearinghouse that helps match individuals with the projects that need them most.

Make a Difference Every Day

Apart from what you offer to organizations, make a special effort to help individuals who need you a lot. Try to give to your friends and others at least as much as you would give to your family if you were married. Never let yourself believe—not even for a minute—that you can't make someone's life brighter just because you haven't married. You need only to remember how much you have appreciated many little things done for you to realize how much of a difference you can make by doing the same sorts of things for others. If you worry that, because you're single, you won't be able to make as much of a contribution to the world as you would if you were married and had children, resolve this minute to do something nice every single day for someone else. Better still, resolve to do something nice daily for someone who can't reward you (which, of course, rules out all of the people you are romantically involved with). Life holds far lesser accomplishments than that of always being the person who tries to think of others. So send the card, give the gift, offer the help, and say the kind word —and withhold the unkind or mean-spirited one. How many more chances will you *get* to send your grandmother flowers on her birthday? Rejoice when people ask for your help with a project or a move. They aren't asking you for a favor, they are *doing* you one by allowing you to make yet another contribution to someone's well-being.

It's important, of course, to be as good to the people you don't know as you are to the people you do. Write a letter to the editor, praising a reporter or public official. Thank the bank teller whose cheery smile brightens your every Friday afternoon. Bring flowers to your doorman even when it's not Christmas. Don't throw out the magazines and paperbacks that you've finished reading; take them to a nursing home, a senior citizens' center, or the waiting room of a hospital emergency room. And never forget the destitute people who haven't a fraction of what you do. One man I know found a wonderful way to help the people on the street whom his friends rush by. He always carries in his wallet a package of gift certificates to McDonald's that he distributes to those who look especially down on their luck. "If I gave them money, they might buy alcohol or drugs," he explains. "What they really need is food." You, too, need to find a way to help some of the hundreds of people who haven't had many of the advantages you have.

It's also a good idea to do something nice daily for *yourself.* Even good works can begin to take their toll if you aren't being good to your psyche. So, besides bringing flowers to others, don't forget to bring an occasional bouquet to yourself. During a frenzied day at the office, don't bolt a sandwich at your desk. Get some perspective by taking a long lunch-hour walk along a river or through a park. Or take in an art gallery or concert by street musicians on the steps of the public library. At the end of the day, don't immediately rush from one engagement to the next. Take a few minutes at home to relax, put your feet up, and listen to whatever music most soothes the beast within you. Then call a friend whom you can always count on to buoy your spirits. These are your good old days, and they can be your *great* old days.

Finally . . .

No matter how much or little money you have, or how lofty or lowly your background is, you can fill your life with people who give your life meaning and importance, because they love and need you as much as you love and need them. No less than anybody who's married, you can fill your life with people who will cherish you for richer or poorer and for better or worse. You can welcome into your family people of all ages, races, and interests. And, if you don't always get from life what you want to get, you can always give to it what you want to give, because you will always have in your life people who need your contribution.

As the poets have always known, love makes the world go round. But it isn't just romantic love that keeps the planet in spin. In even the best marriages, passion wanes and is replaced by another kind of affection, less intense but no less enduring. So you always need to keep expanding your capacity to love others, in marriage or outside it. Love isn't where you find it so much as where you create it. What you give, you get.

So the greatest joy of being single *isn't* that of becoming an island unto yourself, needing and needed by no one. Neither is the greatest joy that of being able to acquire more and more possessions that are no substitute for other people.

The greatest joy of being single is rather the knowledge that, whether or not you eventually marry, you can always love and be loved by others, not because of what you have, but because of what you are, and not because you have insulated yourself from others, but because you have made yourself vulnerable to them. Everybody doesn't need to be married, but everybody does need to love and be loved, and to know that his or her existence makes a difference to somebody. As the journalist Maury Levy likes to say: "After all, even the Lone Ranger had Tonto."

Never kid yourself into thinking that your life would be easier if you were married—or that your contribution would be more worth while. A good marriage, no less than a good single life, takes an inconceivable amount of time, work, energy, patience, and humor—not to mention more than a little luck. And there is no guarantee, even so, that your partnership will last. So many marriages face eventual disruption that two people who stay married for a lifetime may someday qualify to have their wedding invitation mounted under glass at the Smithsonian Institution, next to the fossilized dinosaurs' teeth.

If you plan to hold down a job and have children after you marry, you will find yourself physically and emotionally taxed in a way you never dreamed possible. You may go for years at a stretch without ever being able to sleep beyond 7 A.M., because that's when the kids wake up. You may also go for months or years without being able to sleep through the night, splurge on a state-of-the-art camera, or spend Saturday afternoon contemplating the abstract expressionist paintings at a local museum.

Yes, you may have help with the children. But money runs out, baby-sitters quit, and not all parents are willing to share equally in raising their offspring, so you can never really tell how much of the responsibility will fall upon you. So why not cherish the time you have right now to explore all of the possibilities that life holds out? Time will come soon enough when any of those possibilities will cease to exist, either because you get married or because you will take on new responsibilities that will otherwise fill up your life.

What's more, the feeling of being trapped in a bad marriage might be even more depressing than the feeling of being trapped in singlehood (should you happen to enjoy surveys like Comparative Misery 101), simply because a bad marriage is so much harder to get out of. It is, in fact, practically impossible to end a marriage without months of wrenching self-examination and guilt, followed by a brutal divorce in which you find yourself to be losing a large portion of everything that seemed to be important to you, right down to a sweet little souvenir ashtray you picked up at a caravansary in the Caribbean and that your spouse may decide to claim as part of the settlement, in a final, humiliating turn of the screw. And there is no way ever to get out of being the parent of a child—the one thing in life that is absolutely irrevocable. Frankly, I would never want to have to choose between married misery and single misery, either of which can push you over the edge.

So, instead of always looking ahead to the better life that awaits you somewhere else, it makes sense to commit yourself to giving the best that's in you to give to the life you have now. Fix up your apartment. Spend time with people you love. Get out of a romance that the romance has gone out of, or a job that hasn't been right for you for years, and find the one you deserve. And, if you can't be happy, be cheerful and kind. By maintaining an upbeat, optimistic, and gracious outlook on life, you may not solve all your problems, but you at least won't make them worse by giving in to self-pity or by driving away the people who can help you solve them: your friends. Try also to *look* your best, which lifts your spirits along with other people's. You may not be able to solve all your problems, but you can wear them well.

The truth is that you never know what will result from giving your best effort, and especially whether it will result in your getting married or not. But you *do* know what will result from your not giving your best effort: the feeling that you will never know what you could have achieved because you didn't really reach for it.

Try, above all, to do things you couldn't or wouldn't do if you were married or a parent. Join the Peace Corps, run for political office, hike the Long Trail. Go new places and have new adventures—and don't worry so much about how it will all turn out in the end. The journey matters as much as your arrival at a destination. To have an exciting voyage, collect experiences instead of things. Former student activist Sam Brown, a former leader of the so-called "children's crusade" for 1968 presidential candidate Eugene McCarthy, once sold his house to finance a successful campaign for state treasurer of Colorado. Less than a decade later, he admitted that the same sort of effort would today be far more difficult: "Now, I've got two kids, and I'm not prepared to make those kinds of sacrifices." Try to think of what sacrifices you, too, might never be willing to make again.

However young or old you are, and however much you do or don't want to wed, you need goals in life besides getting married and having children. A lot has changed for single people and others, but the one thing that hasn't changed is simply this: to be human is to be at times alone, and to fight being alone is to fight nothing less than life itself. Solitude may come less often in marriage but brings no fewer challenges. As Lily Tomlin likes to say, "Remember, we're all in this together by ourselves." So don't wait for somebody else to give your life a meaning and direction only you can supply. As a single man or woman, you have a choice: you can put your life on ice while you wait for the wholesale changes that make life worthwhile, or you can keep constantly making retail changes until you bring your life to where you want it to be, with or without a spouse.

Overwhelmingly, the happiest single people choose the second approach. They know that there exist no happy lives, only happy moments. But, by filling your life with as many happy moments as you can, you will always be able to look back on a life that has had more good times than bad— and that makes all the difference. A character named Ben Griggs makes the following speech, regretting the missed opportunities of his life, in Lillian Hellman's play *The Autumn Garden:*

> "So at any given moment you're only the sum of your life up to then. There are no big moments you can reach unless you've a pile of smaller moments to stand on. That big hour of decision, the turning point in your life, the someday you've counted on when you'd suddenly wipe out your past mistakes, do the work you'd never done, think the way you'd never thought, have what you'd never had—it just doesn't come suddenly. You've trained yourself for it while you waited—or you've let it all run past you and frittered yourself away."

With or without a partner, you have a unique, creative, and important gift to give to the world and the people in it. That gift is the gift of your best self, and it is one that is all the easier to give when you have created a firm pedestal on which to stand: a home, a faith, a secure financial future, and friends of many ages and interests.

The truth is that you can never tell if or when marriage will beckon. You can fritter away years chasing a partner at every turn, only to find that you never link up with one. Or you can go your own way, allowing marriage to take the hindmost, and find a spouse almost in spite of yourself. In singlehood, as in life, you never can tell.

But, if you can't predict whether or not you will marry, you can predict what will happen if you don't move forward in some way right now. As Will Rogers said: "Even if you're on the right track, you'll get run over if you just sit there."

Single people today, whether they are unmarried by chance or by choice, have an unprecedented opportunity to lay claim to all the freedom that their marital status can offer. As an unattached man or woman, you can produce, direct, stage-manage, and star in your own show. You can even write your own review, because what matters is not whether someone else enjoys the play but only whether you do.

The only catch is that the curtain has already risen, so you are always creating your own work in progress. Your stage is set, and it is yours to cross timidly and fearfully—or to stride across boldly and with joy, knowing that for every obstacle there exists a corresponding opportunity, and for every pitfall a pleasure. Whether you have walked onto that stage willingly or not, nobody else can replace you on it. It's your show, and it can be one that excites and delights you, married or not.

Ready or not: here life comes, day in and day out, every *single* day.

Index

ABOUT THE AUTHOR

Janice Harayda is a Boston-based journalist and editor who has been writing about single people since the early 1970s, when she received her first by-line in a national magazine for an article about her experiences in singles bars. She was the book critic for *Glamour* and edited the magazine's popular "How to Do Anything Better Guide." A winner of *Mademoiselle*'s Guest Editor competition, she has also worked for *Saturday Review*. Her articles have appeared in *Money, Seventeen, Reader's Digest, Newsday,* the New York *Times,* the *Christian Science Monitor, Working Woman,* and many other publications. A native of North Brunswick, N.J., she attended the University of New Hampshire, and will soon begin graduate study at Harvard University. She lives on Beacon Hill, near the former homes of such notable singles as Henry James and Louisa May Alcott.